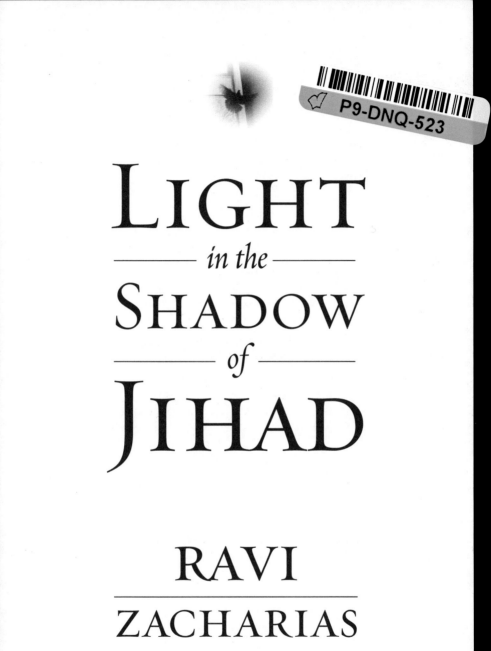

LIGHT

in the

SHADOW

of

JIHAD

RAVI
ZACHARIAS

Multnomah®Publishers *Sisters, Oregon*

LIGHT IN THE SHADOW OF JIHAD
published by Multnomah Publishers, Inc.

published in association with the literary agency of
Wolgemuth & Associates, Inc., 8600 Crestgate Circle, Orlando, FL 32819

© 2002 by Ravi Zacharias
International Standard Book Number: 1-57673-989-9

Cover images by Photodisc

Unless otherwise indicated, Scripture quotations are from:
The Holy Bible, New International Version
© 1973, 1984 by International Bible Society,
used by permission of Zondervan Publishing House

Other Scripture quotations are from:
The Holy Bible, King James Version (KJV)

Multnomah is a trademark of Multnomah Publishers, Inc.,
and is registered in the U.S. Patent and Trademark Office.
The colophon is a trademark of Multnomah Publishers, Inc.

Printed in the United States of America

For information:
MULTNOMAH PUBLISHERS, INC.
POST OFFICE BOX 1720
SISTERS, OREGON 97759

02 03 04 05 06 07 08—10 9 8 7 6 5 4 3 2 1 0

To the Land that I love

CONTENTS

A HAND *from the* RUBBLE

Every time I revisit the collapse of the World Trade Center, whether on screen or in memory, my head shakes irresistibly at the incredible sight, and my heart quivers with overwhelming grief. Like two giants struck at the knees, the buildings buckle and implode with a deafening roar, drowning out the cries and screams of thousands, the debris soaring into a mushroom cloud of rancid, black smoke.

Those fortunate enough to flee through the storm of carnage on that day felt a different torment. They were rained upon not only by bits of concrete and steel, but also by the heart-sickening mix of shredded human bodies disseminated into that cloudburst of devastation.

The world came to a standstill. How can we ever forget it? September 11 or 9/11 is forever etched into our consciences. This dastardly act of mass murder by a handful of brutes has terrifyingly reminded us of the hell that a mind and will devoid of conscience can unleash upon the world.

Now, as I write, while the dying embers still burn amid the ruins, a firestorm of questions rage within our hearts. Different investigative agencies may ask different questions, and they must. But every thinking human being struggles with the questions behind the questions, and we must. Those questions may be few, but they are all-encompassing. They may be age-old, but they are painfully immediate. They may be sensitized by cultural and religious differences, but they cannot be ignored. They may cut across age and education lines, but they are personal. They may divide us in the search for answers, but those answers, rightly plumbed, are the only things that can unite us.

Where does one begin? I have read and heard the common refrain: Why do they hate us? Is it our foreign policy? Had we been there after the Soviet Union pulled out of Afghanistan, could we have prevented this? Is it the poverty? (No one asked these questions when the demagogues at whose behest this happened slaughtered their own poor and helpless by the thousands.)

All these inquiries are important, but at best they touch the surface. When we get to the deeper questions that we must ask, the real discomfort begins. Is this Islam at work or is it its abuse? What does this portend for the future? Is this the inevitable result of religion? If so, what does it tell us of the place of religion in public life? How is it that a God of love allows these things to happen; and if indeed He does, who is this God anyway? Why do we call evil what the perpetrators call good? Who decides those categories?

These questions are evidence that, as much as we seek and need political and military help, we are dazed by the monumental nature of the challenge. Perhaps the truest statement that has been uttered is that this is a different type of war. It is true in more ways than one. Why is this war so different? After all, we read of killings on a daily basis. We have been subjected to school shootings, office workers going on a killing spree, letter bombs, and so on. Indeed, we regularly read of random acts of terror in various parts of the world and return quickly to our normal lives. Until now we have been convinced that somehow it was not *our* problem. It was not *our* children's school or *our* loved one's office, and so it has not been personal for most of us.

But now something strange has happened. The World Trade Center, the symbol of multinational prosperity, and the Pentagon, the symbol of national security, were in a moment smashed by our own instruments in the hands of people who lived among us, scheming our destruction. In a strange way, this has now become *our* war—every one of us has been attacked. We can no longer say it is not our problem.

Some years ago, I watched the excellent movie *Shenandoah*, set during the American Civil War. The lead character is Pa Anderson, played inimitably by James Stewart. The Anderson family, living in Virginia, is determined not to be drawn into the war. Pa Anderson has a farm to take care of and a family to raise. He is not going to send his sons and daughters into this war that does not concern him. He just wants to be left alone. As the sounds of gunfire get closer and closer, officers in the militia appear more frequently at his door, asking the young men to join their ranks. Each time, the determined and hard-nosed Anderson reminds the officers that these boys are *his* sons and not the state's, and no one is going to drag them into this conflict. This is not his battle.

But one day, the apple of his eye—his youngest son—is mistakenly identified as a Confederate soldier and taken captive by a marauding Union troop. When a young servant boy comes running and breaks the news to Pa Anderson, his face twists with anger and then his shoulders drop with resignation. He gathers the rest of his boys and saddles the horses in pursuit of his youngest. That pursuit begins with the words, "Now we are in it. Now it is our war."

America is now in it. We are in a struggle for

survival, and we face an uncertain future before a cruel and ultimately homeless enemy. He is everywhere and he does not have to be great in number in order to be terrifying. He borrows from our own resources and uses our lifestyle and culture to destroy both. In short, we live with vulnerability because of our strength. Just as the weight of a giant can be used against him, so we seem fearful to make a move lest we fall because of our size.

Branding this a different kind of war causes it to take on a meaning we may not yet fathom. Having received a staggering blow that awakened us from our illusion of security, we must now ask who we are as a people. What makes this nation what it is? What do we as a people really believe about life and death? How we answer these most basic questions will determine whether we stand or fall. Though our political and military leaders can offer solutions, they will not provide the ultimate answers. For those we must go deeper.

At the same time, I am optimistic that the terror stalking us can also be used against those who seek to make us fearful. How is that possible, one might ask?

A few years ago, I was in Washington for a discussion on anti-American sentiment and the persecution of Christians, particularly in Islamic countries. During the roundtable discussion, Peggy Noonan, the writer and newspaper columnist, asked,

"Is there anything these persecutors fear?" I attempted to answer her with two brief responses.

First, yes, there is something they fear—a morally strong America. They firmly believe that an America with no moral convictions can easily be run into the ground. But an America that has deep moral convictions is formidable. America, at its core, is a nation birthed in a faith in God. The American people must, therefore, defend their cause with transcendent purpose.

Second, as much as we need a healthy fear of what those who hate America can use against us, we must with equal awareness consider the ridicule that genuine faith in God suffers in this country at the hands of radical academics *among us* who have tossed out the Creator in our national ethos and worldview. That eviction has fearsome and drastic implications, emasculating the country of its essential strength. Our moral strength and spiritual commitment will determine our future.

But that very assertion demands an explanation. And that is what this book is about. Answers do not come in isolation. They come built upon other answers, which had better be right.

During my graduate studies, I took a course in which half the grade depended upon the answers we gave on the exams, while the other half was based upon the questions we asked in the class. The professor was a firm believer in the value of asking the right questions. If there is a sliver of light in the darkness of this hour, it is in the fact that we are asking the right questions.

People accustomed to living in caves, who claim to shun the spires and successes of our world, have thrust those questions upon us. They believe their way of thinking and ruling is what their god had in mind for humanity. They call it *jihad*. The term literally means "struggle." The extremists argue that jihad is "all-out warfare." The moderates contend that it is nothing more than the struggle of the soul. If the latter is the case, this is a form of jihad that applies to both the attacker and the attacked. How we succeed in this struggle will either yield light or spread the darkness.

I believe that the answers to the questions that have been prompted by this event will reveal not just a sliver of light to us, but the bright daybreak of conviction, hope, and meaning, which are worth living for and dying for.

Thirty-three-year-old Genelle Guzman was the last person to be rescued from what has become known as Ground Zero. She had been buried under the rubble for twenty-seven hours, her legs caught between felled pillars and her head trapped in a stack of concrete. During that time, she swung between moments of prayer and utter despair. As night came, she finally fell asleep out of sheer exhaustion. She somehow survived the night, and as dawn broke she heard voices. At midday, with hope dying but her will to live still fighting, she mustered all her energy and called out for help. She clawed desperately through the rubble until somebody finally heard her voice and the sounds of her feeble attempts to free herself. In a final, valiant attempt, she thrust a bruised and battered hand through the mountain of debris that had buried her. Suddenly, she felt a hand clasp hers and in gratefulness she cried out, "Thank God, Thank God!"

Genelle's experience may well be the metaphor from which we can draw our own hope. The strong hand of faith can pull us from the darkness of the rubble of hate and violence we now find ourselves in.

That is my prayer and hope. A struggle it will be. But isn't that what epitomizes life most? What is even more certain is that it is a battle that can be won.

CHAPTER TWO

THE STRUGGLE
between GOOD *and* EVIL

"This is a war between good and evil."

W e heard those words within hours of the attack on America. The country stood united, and there was no doubt that the wickedness of what had been done had pierced the conscience of the vast majority of people. Journalists and politicians were driven to tears. Something that defied reason had taken place. Sadness, like a cloud, enveloped our emotions.

And then we began to hear and see reactions from around the world. While most grieved at the horror, the camera showed others dancing in the streets. To them, the destruction was a feast for the eyes, and they distributed sweets to celebrate this disorienting blow to America's tranquility. It was but a few days before the words broke from one reporter's lips, "One man's terrorist is another man's freedom fighter."

How do we make sense of all this? Politics took over center stage, and suddenly it seemed as though this was payback time for us. The politicization of morality is not a new thing; it has always been a safe haven for any kind of act or behavior. If I am able to find political justification for anything I think or do, my thoughts or actions can be deemed morally right.

We are all tempted to justify our proclivities with political arguments. On the one hand, those of us who are privileged to live in democracies have convinced ourselves that morality is purely a private matter, and we allow no one to invade that territory. Sit in on the lectures of some intellectual arguing from the liberal side of any issue and it becomes clear that relativism is the guide writ large on our cultural belief. We hear it said that there is no such thing as an absolute and that each one must decide his or her moral lifestyle. Anyone who holds to absolutes is mocked and derided.

On the other hand, demagogues such as Osama bin Laden believe that morality is a totally public matter, interwoven with religion, and that their followers are doing the world a favor by ridding it of any culture that privatizes religion and morality. I can just picture bin Laden's diatribes as he speaks to his suicide squads. Every word must drip with conviction that their mission is necessary to "save the world." Anything and everything is justified by his ultimate goal of killing those who stand in the way of the greater good of a totalitarian religion.

Yet, if we pierce the armor of both extremes, we find very quickly what lies beneath. The relativist who argues for the absence of absolutes smuggles absolutes into his arguments all the time, while shouting loudly that all morality is private belief. Alan Dershowitz, professor at Harvard Law School, spares no vitriol in his pronouncements that there are no absolutes and that that's the way it is. "I do not know what is right," he contends. It all sounds very honest and real, until he points his finger at his audience and says, "And you know what? Neither do you." So it is not just that he does not know what is right. It is also that he knows the impossibility of knowing what is right so well that he is absolutely certain that nobody else can know what is right either. There is his absolute. One need only observe his tirades and his views on numerous issues, including his vociferous defense of O. J. Simpson during his murder trial, to see how relativism works itself into society's ethics.

Then you go to the other extreme. On the night before Mohammed Atta and his band of murderers brought the world to a screaming halt with their suicide mission to "rid the world of American values," these specimens of "moral rectitude" were parked in nude dance clubs, in search of the services of a prostitute. What hypocrisy littered their moral pronouncements! Lies, deceit, sensuality, illegal acts, fake passports, mass murder—all in defense of absolutes.

In the face of such duplicity, how do we recognize right and wrong? In the rubble of human failure and destruction, how do we connect with a helping hand to rescue us from falsehood?

THE STEPPING STONE OF INTUITION

Rarely have I met a true relativist. Hidden somewhere in the words of everyone who argues for complete relativism is a belief that there are, indeed, some acts that are wrong. The bottom line is this: When someone says that all truth is relative, he or she is making either a relative statement or an absolute one. If it is a relative statement, then that statement, by definition, is not always true. On the other hand, if the belief that all truth is relative is absolute, the very statement itself must be denied, because it denies absolutes. The pure relativist cuts off the branch on which he is sitting while telling you the branch cannot be severed. The landing is mind shattering.

In his book *Into Thin Air*, Jon Krakauer relates the experience of the climbers of Mount Everest in that

1996 expedition that ended up costing the lives of many. One of the chilling stories he recounts is of one group that had just been rescued by another, so that they were able to continue their journey upward. A few hundred feet later, the group that had been rescued now had the opportunity to save the lives of the climbers who had helped them. But rather than risk their own lives, they pressed onward, leaving them to perish. Later, when they had descended the mountain and were asked why they had ignored the plight of these others, their crisp answer was, "Above eight-thousand meters there is no morality."

Once when I was speaking at Oxford University, a small group of students came up to me afterward and insisted that good and bad were not absolute categories. I asked one of them whether it would be wrong for me to take a butcher knife and cut to pieces a one-year-old child for sheer delight. There was a pause, and then he said, to an audible gasp from those listening, "I would not like what you did, but I could not honestly say that it would be wrong."

The relativist is never comfortable on the receiving end of his own assumptions. At best, he denies himself the right to any moral pronouncement; yet he cringes at the implications. And that is the point. Even when absolutes are denied, there is an intuitive certainty that some things are just plainly wrong. Alan Dershowitz,

who denies our ability to define good, says with equal
vehemence that he does recognize evil when he sees it.
Fascinating!

And so we go back to our nemesis in Afghanistan,
bin Laden, who applauded the killing of thousands in
the World Trade Center. Is it not ironic that when the
American forces retaliated with their bombing mission,
he and his supporters in the Taliban appealed to the
conscience of the world by saying that innocent
civilians (some of whom may have been relatives or
friends) were being killed? These very people, who have
killed tens of thousands of their own, were suddenly
worrying about civilians? When the killing affects the
ones they love, then it becomes morally wrong.

One of the saddest stories to emerge from the
media coverage of the Taliban's control over
Afghanistan was a report from an Afghan village,
where an old man sat, his face in his hands, just staring
into the sand. That picture said it all. His village had
been ravaged and raped by Taliban fighters. His son
had been skinned like an animal, and his skeletal
remains lay buried in a shallow grave. The sight was
nauseating.

Is it any wonder that the old man sat alone in the
desert with an expression of unbearable and word-
suffocating grief? What was there left to say or to do?
Why would anyone want to live, if that is what living

meant? To whom do you express your numbing heartache? What kind of mind-set did these murderers have to distribute such a hell? Evil was clearly recognizable in its merciless slaughter, even across cultural boundaries. Whether at eight-thousand meters, or high atop a building, or in the desert, evil looks hideous because the receiving end is always Ground Zero.

That is our first clue. It does not matter whether evil comes from the hand of a proclaimed absolutist or a relativist. Evil, plainly stated, is the destruction of what life was essentially meant to be. That is the simplest way to begin. And so, on that fateful day, airplanes built for safe travel were commandeered by diabolical men and smashed into buildings. Buildings erected for the safety of those within were turned into infernos. Entry permits were given to these men with the expectation that they would live by the laws of the land, not destroy its people. Intended purpose was violated in each case, and destruction was the result.

But this is where the issue begins to get clouded, does it not? Someone might say that the airline and the passengers had one purpose, but the terrorists had another. So how can we define evil as merely the destruction of purpose? "Whose purpose?" we might ask.

The Uncertain Footing of Reason

We move, then, from intuition as a stepping-stone to the building block of reason. In intuition we at least saw one sliver of light. When we love somebody, the destruction of that life is evil in our eyes. But what do we do with evil on a grander scale; with evil that does not touch us directly? Here we suddenly run aground.

Contrary to what relativists espouse, reason alone cannot help us sort things out. Bertrand Russell, that great voice for life without God, confessed when discussing how ethical values could be judged, "I don't know the solution." The noted Canadian atheist Kai Neilsen said:

> We have been unable to show that Reason requires the moral point of view, or that really rational persons...need not be egoists or classical amoralists. Reason doesn't decide here. The picture I have painted for you is not a pleasant one. Reflection on it depresses me.... Pure practical reason, even with a good knowledge of the facts, will not take you to morality.[1]

Do you hear what Neilsen is saying? Reason cannot lead you to morality. Reason cannot argue against an amoral or egoistic lifestyle. One cannot call upon sheer rationality to argue for an "ought" in life. This is the prison of secular reasoning. This is the dead end of "one man's terrorist is another man's freedom fighter." This is the voice of the student saying, "I would not like it, but I cannot call it morally wrong." This is America's quandary. How do we determine what is evil? Do we do so intuitively or rationally, when one is so personal and the other so beyond reason?

Let me take you one step further. Ultra-rationalists tell you not only that reason cannot lead you to morality; they tell you that your very hope for moral reasoning is irrational. Listen to the words of Richard Dawkins from Oxford:

> In a universe of blind physical forces and genetic replication, some people are going to get hurt, and other people are going to get lucky; and you won't find any rhyme or reasoning to it, nor any justice. The universe we observe has precisely the properties we should expect if there is at the bottom, no design, no purpose, no evil, and no good. Nothing but blind, pitiless indifference. DNA neither knows nor cares. DNA just is. And we dance to its music.[2]

Do you see what he is saying? Is he saying that the moralist is rationally wrong-headed because there is no such thing as good? Indeed! But he is saying more. Even the likes of Alan Dershowitz, who does not believe that we know what is right, is also wrong, says Dawkins, because Dershowitz at least believes that evil is recognizable. But according to Dawkins, there is no such thing as evil either. In short, no good, no evil. We are all just dancing to our DNA, and DNA neither knows nor cares. Mohammed Atta was dancing to his DNA. Bin Laden is dancing to his DNA.

Tell that to the old man in Afghanistan, weeping over the skinning of his son. Tell that to the children whose dads and moms are not coming home because of September 11. Tell them there is no good or evil. This universe is just a blind, pitiless existence, and so let them dance to its tune.

And forget justice, because that does not exist either. Maybe that is why Bertrand Russell and Albert Einstein issued a joint statement two days before Einstein died: "Those of us who know the most are the gloomiest about the future." Knowledge without morality is deadly.

Such is the world of reason—unhinged from any ultimate purpose in life. This is the terrifying reality we face in a world of thinkers who think thinking is bereft of an ultimate thinker. This is the world of persons who believe that there is no ultimate person to whom personhood can look. This is the world of warfare among ideas, where good and bad are vacuous terms. Maybe bin Laden has unwittingly called the bluff of rationalists and shown them what a world without good and evil would be like.

THE CORNERSTONE OF VALUE

What, then, must the average person do, caught in the trap of reason but clinging to the lifeline of intuition? There is only one hope. That hope was penned into the American Declaration of Independence as the rock on which the surefootedness of our value as humans stands:

> We hold these truths to be self-evident, that all men are created equal, that they are endowed by their Creator with certain unalienable rights, that among these are life, liberty and the pursuit of happiness.

That one sentence sets America apart from most of the nations of the earth. Our value is not derived from government benevolence or from the mercies of democracy. Democracy and individual dignity derive from the transcendent reality of a Creator. Take away the Creator, and we are at the mercy of the powers of the moment.

This is vital to our understanding for the future. We can debate from now till the end of the world whether America is a Christian nation. The certainty is this: America was not founded on an Islamic, Hindu, or Buddhist worldview, however valuable some of their precepts might be. If we do not see this, we do not see the fundamental ideas that shaped the ethos of the American people. In that sense, bin Laden has a better understanding of us than we have of ourselves. Only within the Christian framework could a nation have been conceived that recognizes that God Himself has bestowed intrinsic dignity upon us. We are not the result of natural causes, but of a supernatural one. We are individuals with dignity in essence; and freedom, even with its risks, has been endowed upon us by our Creator.

But with that recognition comes a responsibility. Reason and intuition are pointers to the need for morality, but it is only on the character of God that morality is based. Just as God cannot self-destruct because He is pure goodness, so in drawing from His character we can avoid the breakdown of our own lives and the destruction of our purpose. God provides the blueprint of what life was intended to be. He not only shows us in His commands what we must do, but in His person what it is to *be.* He clothes us with dignity and guards the dignity of everyone, regardless of origin or creed. Freedom is given but tempered by mutual respect and justice. Government is established to maintain order, but authorities are to guard against abuse. Laws are made but with the backdrop of civility and safety. The family is affirmed as the sacred trust of the parents. Children are honored as models of faith and tenderness. A moral framework is the heart of any nation's belief, because in that moral framework the value of a person is defined. Worship is the glue that binds life together.

Those very beliefs have shaped our national affinities. America has a natural fraternity with countries that uphold such moral precepts. And all of those countries base their fundamental worldview on Judeo-Christian assumptions. The four cities that converged in the making of America were Jerusalem, Athens, Rome, and London. Jerusalem framed the moral conscience; Rome, the legal framework; Athens, the philosophical backdrop; and London, the cultural ethos that carried over into America's infant years. Is it any surprise that those very nations today, principally Israel and the United Kingdom, stand in such close relationship with the United States?

This relationship is often misrepresented as being only politically driven. But the affinity between these nations goes deeper and is born out of shared values in the first place. It is a bond that comes from a shared worldview—the fundamental tenet that life is intrinsically sacred—though there may be significant diversity over specific doctrines.

Therein lies the defining distinctive: Life is intrinsically sacred because God created it. There is no other way to convey intrinsic sanctity. It cannot be conveyed by human ingenuity or by the passing of a law. This truth is as essential a part of my being as the very life within me—it frames my entire moral outlook.

"But just a minute," you might say. "Doesn't Islam also have a created order?"

I shall address this more fully later, but for now, I will only say that the teachings of Islam go beyond a created order to a geo-political theory. It was conceived on certain socio-economic and legal or judicial dictates that were never, ever in the American frame of reference. (I could list a number of them, but that is not the purpose of this argument.) When the framers of the Declaration of Independence and the writers of the Constitution referred to God, they did not envision pantheism, where man is divine, or the theocracy of Islam, where religious belief is a compulsion.

In short, America functions within a moral framework, and that framework can be meaningful only when attached to a Creator. This was the very reason that George Washington, in his farewell address, warned his country against any attempt to build a moral framework apart from God:

Of all the disputations and habits that lead to political prosperity, religion and morality are indispensable supports. In vain would that man claim the tribute of patriotism who should labor to subvert these great pillars of human happiness—These finest props of duties of men and citizens.... And let us with caution indulge the supposition that morality can be maintained without religion. Whatever may be conceded to the influence of refined education on the minds of peculiar structure, reason and experience, both forbid us to expect that national morality can prevail in exclusion of religious principle.

I want to underscore two principal thoughts from those profound words, spoken over two-hundred years ago. Washington said, "Let us with caution indulge the supposition that morality can be maintained without religion." He must have anticipated that an effort would be made to base morality on something other than a religious worldview. He warned us of the treacherous terrain we would embark upon in such a venture. Those academics who want to take us on this journey are risking the future of America. They are flirting with the ultimate danger of destruction of purpose. Life is sacred and the particulars will disintegrate if the basis for them is destroyed.

Washington's second warning—that reason and experience forbid us to expect morality to prevail if religion is excluded—was also prophetic. In a strange paradox, many who come to America's shores, even from other religious backgrounds, choose to send their children to Christian schools rather than to public schools, because they want a moral basis for their children's education. They know the strength of morality and the weakness of naturalistic assumptions.

In our struggle to find a light for morality in the shadow of destruction, let us find the purpose that comes only from God. The closing paragraph of the Declaration of Independence begins "We, therefore, the Representatives of the United States of America, in General Congress assembled, appealing to the Supreme Judge of the world...." and ends with the words: "And for the support of this declaration, with a firm reliance on the protection of Divine providence, we mutually pledge to each other our lives, our fortunes, and our sacred honor."

Sacredness of life and the protection of God are woven into the fabric of our national existence. Without that recognition the words of freedom ring hollow.

September 11 may be a clarion call to America to realize that the fight ahead cannot be won by might alone, but by the strength of America's soul.

We must choose between an amoral world and a world that acknowledges a moral basis for life itself, which can only be rooted in God. He gives us our purpose, and any violation of that will breed evil. The famed American essayist and poet James Russell Lowell wrote:

> *Once to every man and nation*
> *comes the moment to decide*
>
> *In the strife of truth with falsehood,*
> *for the good or evil side,*
>
> *With each choice God speaking to us,*
> *offers each the bloom or blight*
>
> *Then the man or nation chooses*
> *for the darkness or the light.*

In the shadow of jihad, our moral basis for existence will be tested first.

CHAPTER THREE

THE STRUGGLE *between* TRUTH *and* FALSEHOOD

Growing up in India, I heard the old illustration of an Englishman asking for directions on a crowded street in New Delhi. The Indian just looked at his questioner and shrugged, while muttering, "Sorry, no speak English." The exasperated Englishman repeated himself, only this time louder than before, as if his volume could compensate for the listener's linguistic limitation.

We are in a similar quandary when we ask the question, "Is this terrorist act Islam at work, or the abuse of it?" If we were to ask the perpetrators of the act, they would say they were about Allah's business. Yet other Muslims roundly reject that assertion and castigate these individuals as enemies of Islam. If those who are immersed in the religion have such diametrically opposed views, what chance does an outsider have to find the answer to that question? One might contend that all we need to do is read the Koran, but Muslims claim that the only way to understand the true meaning of the Koran is to read it in Arabic. No translation is given the authority that the original has. In the context of the illustration at the beginning, shouting louder will not solve the problem.

To further complicate matters, it does not help to talk with those scholars from within the Islamic world who take issue with Islam because of their fear of reprisal. Thus those who speak in defense of radical Islam give us one view. Those who disagree do so at their life's peril. Those who quote the Koran but do not know Arabic are discounted as ignorant of the religion. Any attempt to discuss the historical backdrop threatens offense.

Where does that leave us? As the world teeters on the brink of a worldwide conflagration, the bulk of us do not know what we are fighting. Are terrorist acts part and parcel of Islam or the distortion of it?

In this chapter I will lay out the basis the contending factions give for their positions; then we can make our own judgment on whether the weight of evidence is on one side or the other. Whatever else we do, we must know the truth and respond in courteous and peaceable ways.

Many factors led to the dreadful events of September 11. Political, social, economic, and cultural issues were at play. We need only look at the pitiful conditions under which millions in Muslim countries live to see how easy it would be to sway them into suicide missions and other life-threatening actions. As I ponder the deprived lot of so many, I cannot help but think of France two-hundred years ago, when the common person rose up in revolt. Charles Dickens well described that fervor on the eve of the French Revolution: "Here splendor rode hard on the bony shoulders of squalor.... Till humanity long crushed rose up with that awful monstrosity called the guillotine."

Such realities do play a part in desperate and dreadful acts. But we would be naïve and highly prejudiced to think that this alone explains it. Poverty only provides the context. The beliefs drilled into the minds of the masses in this movement orchestrated by bin Laden provide the soil and the impetus. The religious foundation is key. If there is intransigence in the religious aspect, it does not matter what other factors change; religion will still shape the mind-set of a horde of people.

The Birth of Islam

Islam came to birth through the visions and revelations claimed by its prophet, Muhammad, who was born in A.D. 570 At the age of twenty-five he was commissioned from being a keeper of camels to take charge of the business affairs of a wealthy widow, fifteen years his senior. She was impressed by his character and soon proposed marriage to him. Although after she died he took numerous wives, while she was alive, she remained his only wife.

At the age of forty he began to retire into a cave for extensive periods of contemplation and meditation. After one of these occasions he told his wife that he had been visited by an angel who ordered him "to recite," and from that command came the Koran, which literally means, "to recite." At first he was perplexed by it all, but his wife told him this could well be the call of God upon him. She became his first follower, and then a handful of family members followed suit. Many resisted his claim to be God's spokesman, and it was only after various battles, arguments, and wars that Muhammad was able to gain the following of a vast number in Arabia. In the first one hundred years of this movement, numerous capitals, such as Jerusalem, Damascus, and Cairo, fell to Islam.

The succession to Muhammad after his unexpected death in A.D. 632 became a serious, divisive issue, as he had not named a successor. An immediate struggle for the leadership ensued. One group, the Sunnis, insisted that the first caliph should be elected.

Shia'hs or Shi'ites argued that the successor must come from Muhammad's own bloodline, which would have been Ali, his cousin and son-in-law. Although there are several other sects in Islam today, these two form the principal bodies.

Three of the first four caliphs were assassinated. It was under the third caliphate of Uthman that any variant readings of the Koran were burned. This spurred critics within Islam to charge that the text had been tampered with. This debate still rages.

In its formative centuries, while Islam solidified as a religious and political entity, a large body of interpretive literature was developed to explain the Koran. The most important composition is the Hadith, the collected sayings and deeds of Muhammad. As well, there is the Sunna, which is the body of Islamic social and legal customs; the Sira, or biographies of Muhammad; and the Tafsir, which is Koranic commentary or explanation. All accounts of the Koran and the early years of Islam are derived from these sources, compiled and written mostly from the mideighth to the midtenth centuries. And it is here that the deepest differences lie, for the sects differ in how much importance they place on each source.

It is not my purpose to go further into a detailed discussion of Islam's origins, but I believe it is important to note the various historical points of division within its ranks that underscore why it is so hard to find a single-mindedness in its methods and goals.

THE ABSOLUTE OR THE RELATIVE IN ISLAM?

One can see the problems developing. First was the problem of succession. Second is the problem of authority. How does one decide which writings are authoritative and which are not? Here, two very significant realities take over.

First is the doctrine of *abrogation*. This is how one scholar describes that doctrine:

> The Koran is unique among sacred Scriptures in teaching a doctrine according to which later pronouncements of the prophet abrogate, i.e., declare null and void, his earlier pronouncements. The importance of knowing which verses abrogate others has given rise to the Kor'anic science known as Nasikh wa Mansukh, the Abrogators and the Abrogated.[3]

This doctrine is based on the verse in the Koran which Muhammad himself uttered about later revelations superceding former ones.[4] Leading Islamic commentators see no problem with this, although the rest of us might well be puzzled. If the Koran is declared to be a perfect revelation, what is the doctrine of abrogation saying except that all absolutes are relative to the moment? If that is so, how does one arbitrate between the extremists who use some passages from the Koran and the Hadith to justify mass murder and those who say that Muhammad abrogated the original command?

The most often quoted passage on the use of force in world-domination is the *ayatus-saif*, which literally means "the verse of the sword." Surah 9.5 says, "But when the forbidden months are past, then fight and slay the pagans wherever ye find them, and seize them, beleaguer them, and lie in wait for them in every stratagem (of war)."

While some use this passage to defend the sword in Islam, others counter that this is taken out of context. But the extremists quickly argue that this is not all they have in their defense. They recount the incident, cited by one of Muhammad's biographers, in which their prophet oversaw the slaughter of hundreds of his enemies in Medina: "The apostle of Allah, may Allah bless him, sat with his companions and they were brought in small groups. Their heads were struck off. They were between six hundred and seven hundred in number."[5]

Even the arch defenders of Muhammad's character take a step back at this point. One of them says, "But by any but that standard of morality and by his own conspicuous magnanimity on other occasions, his act in all its accessories was one of cold-blooded murder."[6]

We can readily see that within Islamic groups there are those who take one angle, and some, another. Those who defend militancy cite two other passages. Muhammad himself, after various conquests, wrote from Medina to both Caesar in Rome and Chosroes in Persia, saying, "Submit or suffer consequences." When he wrote the Treaty of Medina, he divided the people into two categories—*Dar al-Islam* or The House of Islam and *Dar al-Harb*, The House of War. Militants also point to Muhammad's last words: "Umar b. Abd al-Aziz reported that the last statement made by the Apostle of Allah (may peace be upon him) was: 'O Lord, perish the Jews and the Christians…. Beware, there should be no two faiths in Arabia.'"[7]

Those who challenge the violent side, question how Muhammad could ever have uttered those words. Those who defend it, defend the authority of the Tradition and the warfare that was carried on, even in their prophet's lifetime.

THE CONFLICT DEEPENS

The radicals' hostility is often the most severe toward their own dissenters or those within the faith who go "astray." Let me give a critical example of this.

Some years ago many leading Islamic scholars began to call upon Muslims to subject their faith to historical and critical scrutiny. Specifically, their sacred texts needed to be examined. This campaign came to a critical point in 1972 during the renovation of the Great Mosque of Sana'a in Yemen. Mounds of documents and texts were uncovered at that time, which compelled several scholars to begin a critical study of the very sources of the Koran.[8]

Notable scholars such as Ali Dashti from Iran, Nasr Abu Zaid, Egyptian professor of Arabic; Pakistani scholar Fazlur Rahman; Egyptian journalist Farag Foda; Algerian professor of law at the University of Paris Mohammed Arkoun; and Egyptian government minister and university professor Taha Hussein voiced some honest concerns about the texts and their meaning. These devout Muslim men have paid dearly for questioning the authenticity of the primary sources. Ali Dashti mysteriously disappeared during the revolution in Iran. Abu Zaid was branded apostate and forced to flee the country with his wife (she would not have been permitted to remain with him once he was branded apostate). Farag Foda was assassinated, and so runs the list of those silenced by death or fear.[9]

So while they are of the moderating perspective, they are caught between the radicals and the masses who have lived through much deprivation and political turmoil. They are constantly told that their ill-fate is because of the West and its political and social hostility to Islam, and either through ignorance or fear, have tended to be held in sway by the vitriol of the radical demagogues. Extremists have found it easy in these circumstances to stir up hate and create in the masses a "victim" mentality. The mix of deprivation, victimization, and religious fervor becomes volatile, and for some, deadly. Into this mix the West is dragged by some who feel that it has exacerbated the problem, or by radicals who feel that the West is a hotbed for infidels and the sedition of Islam.

But how has this ancient struggle brought on our contemporary crisis? Is there any hope, or are we cast into the deep with no possibility of rescue?

THE KILLERS AND THEIR CAUSE

One of the key figures in the Muslim Brotherhood Movement, spawned several decades ago in Egypt, was Hasan al-Banna. He came to the conclusion that Egyptian and Islamic societies were destroying their culture through a blind imitation of "Infidel Westerners." He and six others joined together to form the Muslim Brotherhood Movement to bring back an alignment of politics and religion, as he believed Islam was meant to be.

A couple of quotes will explain his ideology. "How wise was the man who said: 'Force is the surest way of implementing the right, and how beautiful it is that force and right should march side by side.'"

He considered the early Islamic conquerors to be the blueprint for the Muslim Brotherhood Movement: "Their homes on their saddles and their swords in their hands, and with the clear argument on the tips of their tongues, calling on all mankind to accept one of these three: Islam, Tribute (Jizya) or Combat."[10]

Al-Banna went on to differentiate clearly between Islam and Christianity, drawing from a quote by Jesus Christ: "It is not our fault that (in Islam) politics is part of religion and that Islam includes the rulers and the ruled, for its teaching is not: 'Give to Caesar what is Caesar's and to God what is God's,' but rather: Caesar and what is Caesar's are to the one and only victorious God."

Al-Banna tried to implement this vision in Egypt, and through a series of attempted assassinations and violent moves, was himself assassinated. Following the imprisonment and subsequent release of some of his followers, their hearts were cemented into a "do or die" mentality. The movement that was to emerge from these setbacks took a different tack. Rather than reform the society from within, they would have to escape from it, preferably to the desert, and then after its collapse, return to build it anew. They called it *Al-*

Takfir wa al-Hijrah (Infidelity and Flight). Their method for building an Islamic society was the systematic use of violence and the spread of fear. Their leader claimed that he alone knew the hidden meanings in the Koran, and he vowed to live out its mandates.

One of their acts was to kidnap and execute the minister of religion in Egypt. But this backfired and led to a determined crackdown and the hanging of their ringleader.

At about the same time all this was happening, Muhammad Abd el Salam Farag, a young engineer in Cairo, wrote *The Missing Religious Precept*, a book inspired by the Muslim Brotherhood Movement. The precept that Muslims had forgotten, he said, was the command to jihad, which he considered the most important religious precept in Islam. Farag was the mastermind behind the assassination of Egyptian President Anwar Sadat on October 6, 1981. (That, by the way, is why Sadat's widow said after the September 11 attacks that the same people who killed her husband were behind this carnage.) The movement Farag headed up was called Al-Jihad.

Of Sadat's assassination, Farag said: "I am the principal conspirator in the operation to assassinate the president of the Republic. By this means I wanted to implement the law of the almighty God, to eradicate the rule of the unbeliever. The aim was to establish an Islamic State."[11]

Farag went on to blame the Crusaders, the Communists, and the Zionists for the ills of nations and cultures.

One look at *The Missing Religious Precept* will explain where bin Laden is coming from. If that document is believed by even a handful of men, it is a fearsome thing. It seethes with hate, incites to kill and destroy, calls for the spread of fear among the "backsliders and infidels," for the murder of leaders, for the scorching of a nation's vegetation and its livelihood, and for building absolute fearlessness in its followers. The promise given through it all is that at the end, Islam will conquer and all its opponents will be vanquished.

The landmark events of September 11, 2001, are the outworking of this ideology. As planes plunged into buildings and mass killing took place, fear became dominant. Who knows what else may have been planned that was foiled by the quick thinking of President Bush and his leadership, and by the heroic actions of a few passengers on the plane that crashed in Pennsylvania? Just imagine how the fear would have escalated had planes crashed into the Capitol and the White House. Had they followed Farag's plan as laid out in *The Missing Religious Precept,* newspapers, radio, and television would also have been targeted and used to spread fear and control the population. If it is ever proven that these same terrorists were the source of the anthrax campaign directed at the television stations and newspapers, perhaps that campaign was merely a test balloon for what their ultimate goal would be.

THE COURAGEOUS AND THEIR CALL

All this leads to two sober-minded conclusions. First and foremost, not every Muslim is committed to violence. I am thankful that many have condemned the brutality of the attack on America. They do not want their families to grow up in fear. I was raised near an Islamic community in India, and had numerous friends of that faith. Many were good friends, and they did not advocate or condone violence against non-Muslims.

Second, if we are going to keep this from becoming a struggle of "Us versus Them," I believe firmly that the following question has to be broached without fear in the Islamic community: Does the moderate Muslim have the courage to speak up against the evil of violence threatened upon anyone, anywhere in the world?

When Ayatollah Khomeini called for the death sentence on Salman Rushdie, was Khomeini being a good Muslim or a bad Muslim? If he was being a bad

Muslim, he needs to be denounced by moderate Muslims. The world needs to hear from the moderate Islamic communities. When the blasphemy laws are applied in countries such as Pakistan and non-Muslims are killed, are those keepers of the law being good Muslims or bad ones? The world needs to hear.

When freedoms are so restricted in Islamic countries that no Muslim is allowed to disbelieve in Islam with impunity, is that a good Muslim law or a bad one? The freedom to believe—or not—is one of the most sacred privileges of the human mind. That freedom is taken away in the name of Islam. Is that good or bad? There is no religious freedom in most Islamic countries. Statistics that indicate that Islam is growing are not an accurate reflection of the hearts of the people, because they really have no choice. I had a close friend who was murdered because he became a Christian. Is this not just plain morally wrong? I well remember his sobering words to me shortly before he died: "Brother Ravi, the more I see of the religion of the land of my birth, the more beautiful Jesus Christ looks to me." If that does not provoke the extremists in Islam to take stock, I do not know what will.

It will not do just to focus on whether the September 11 attack is Islam or its abuse. Some soul searching needs to be done in the Islamic world, and two questions need to be answered:

- •What do they really believe Islam teaches?
- •Do they believe that what Islam teaches is really true?

This soul search, by the way, applies to every religion. And any religion not willing to examine itself will gain a following only through intimidation and fear. It then evicts itself from the public square of honest and truthful debate. Graves are the legacy of such beliefs. The need for self-examination was the heart-cry of Islamic scholars such as Ali Dashti and others who had to flee for their lives, just for raising the question of truth.

Is there any hope that such courage will be exhibited at this crucial time, and if so, will it succeed in overcoming the radical expression of Islam? Observing the courage and candor of those who have already tried to raise questions from within the Islamic community, I come to three conclusions.

First, everyone must be given the freedom to believe what is of ultimate worth to them. The coercion of religious faith is an oxymoron. It is then no longer religion but an ideology of compulsion. Even today in Islamic countries, a centuries-old law brought about by the "Pact of Omar" (the second successor to Muhammad) prohibits the building of a church within one thousand meters of a mosque. No new churches can be built or old ones renewed without the permission of the head of state. This is nothing but religious discrimination and oppression. Moderate voices need to speak up now, so that every man, woman, and child may be free to believe without the threat of the sword.

Second, the voices that decry the murders by bin Laden and his gang of killers must also decry the "lesser" evils. Think, for example, of the sixteen Christian worshipers killed in the midst of their Sunday worship in a small church in Pakistan just a few weeks after September 11. Where are the voices of protest now? Oh yes, we hear a well-modulated condemnation by Pakistani leaders, but that same leadership knows that had Christians entered a mosque and killed Muslim worshipers, a nationwide bloodbath would have ensued. The world needs to know what the difference is here and why it is so.

Are the belligerent ones belligerent because their religion calls for such reprisals, or are they belligerent because that is what their spiritual leaders teach them? It is time to ask what is being taught in the mosques on such matters. That will give us some answers as to what is really believed.

Third is a simple question of allegiance. Can America survive if religious intolerance and cultural ideology override the obligations of citizenship? This is a hard question that the Islamic community must answer to set our minds at ease. I believe there is hope. There is hope, because in the pile of verbal rubble, a voice emerges now and then with the courage to say what needs to be said.

Islamic scholar and devout Muslim, Muqtedar Khan, is the director of International Studies and the Center for the Study of Islam and Democracy at Adrian College, Michigan. Mr. Khan has courageously put his finger on the nerve of this social and cultural matter. I had penned my own thoughts on this within days of September 11. (See the Appendix of this little book.) It was heartwarming, therefore, to see some of those thoughts echoed in Mr. Khan's address to the Muslim community, which I quote from at length:

> I am writing this memo to you all with the explicit purpose of inviting you to lead the American Muslim community in soul searching, reflection and reassessment. What happened on September 11th in New York and Washington, DC will forever remain a horrible scar on the history of Islam and humanity. No matter how much we condemn it, and point to the Quran and the Sunnah to argue that Islam forbids the killing of innocent people, the fact remains that

the perpetrators of this crime against humanity have indicated that their actions are sanctioned by Islamic values. The fact that even now several Muslim scholars and thousands of Muslims defend the accused is indicative that not all Muslims believe that the attacks are un-Islamic. This is truly sad....

While we loudly and consistently condemn Israel for its ill treatment of Palestinians we are silent when Muslim regimes abuse the rights of Muslims and slaughter thousands of them. Remember Saddam and his use of chemical weapons against Muslims? Remember the Mujahideen of Afghanistan and their mutual slaughter? Have we ever condemned them for their excesses? Have we demanded international intervention or retribution against them? Do you know how the Saudis treat their minority Shiis? Have we protested the violation of their rights?

Muslims love to live in the US but also love to hate it. Many openly claim that the US is a terrorist state but they continue to live in it. Their decision to live here is testimony that they would rather live here than anywhere else. As an Indian Muslim, I know for sure that nowhere else on earth, including India, will I get the same sense of dignity and respect that I have received in the US. No Muslim country will treat me as well as the US has. If what happened on September 11th had happened in India, the biggest democracy, thousands of Muslims would have been slaughtered in riots on mere suspicion and there would be another slaughter after confirmation.... But [here] hundreds of Americans have gathered around Islamic centers in symbolic gestures of protection and embrace of American Muslims. In many cities Christian congregations have started wearing hijab to identify with fellow Muslim women. In patience and tolerance ordinary Americans have demonstrated their extraordinary virtues.

It is time that we acknowledge that the freedoms we enjoy in the US are more desirable to us than superficial solidarity with the Muslim world.

It is time for soul searching.... How can Islam inspire thousands of youth to dedicate their lives to killing others? We are supposed to invite people to Islam not murder them. The worst exhibition of Islam has happened on our turf. We must take first responsibility to undo the evil it has manifest. This is our mandate, our burden and also our opportunity.[12]

I commend Mr. Khan for this daring and candid article. I recommend that you read the full article, available on his Web site (see the endnote), to understand his views on Islam. I have one suggestion, however. He makes it clear that the dignity demonstrated in the American response to the terrorist attacks would not have been seen in any other country, not even in other democracies. I would like to suggest that the reason America responded the way it did goes beyond a political philosophy. It is the by-product of a Christian worldview. That Christian worldview beckons us to remember who created us; to take note that heaven, not earth, is the eternal city; to respect the disagreements of others and to provide civil and effective ways of debate; to learn from Jesus Christ that we can even love our enemies; and to know that in matters of ultimate destiny, God alone is the judge.

Until those who are not Muslims are free to practice their faith in Muslim countries—and those who seek to become Christians or choose any other faith can do so with impunity—Islam will never be free from the fear it can engender. I pray for such a day, when one's ultimate choice in life can be made without the fear of terror and hate.

I remember as a young lad growing up in India, hearing a popular song in Hindi. It was called "Amar,

Akbar and Antony." Amar is a Hindu name, Akbar, a Muslim name, and Antony a Christian name. The song was a plea to live and let live. Does this mean there is no difference in what each believes? No, it does not. But it does mean that every individual has a fundamental right to be free to choose what he or she believes about God, in any land and under any government. The Christian faith clearly advocates that. The question for the Muslim is, "Does Islam advocate that also?" Until we know, the struggle will not just be internal and spiritual, but global and geo-political.

CHAPTER FOUR

WERE EVENTS SUCH AS THESE PROPHESIED?

S omeone has quipped that prediction is difficult—especially about the future. Yet the human mind craves to break the stranglehold of present knowledge and take captive the future. Which of us has not yearned for the curtain of time to be lifted even for a moment? In antiquity there were many ways to accomplish this goal, from oracles in "sacred" cities, to mediums who claimed to converse with the dead. We can understand both the desire and the gullibility in such matters.

It is surprising, however, that in a world that has supposedly come of age, we still seek strange, and sometimes sinister, powers to predict what lies ahead. But if it is true that there are people with the ability to know the future, where were they on September 10? Shouldn't one of them have been able to warn our national security agencies of what was to come? And if they did know the events about to take place and did not alert us, what does it say of their culpability?

But God knew, didn't He? Why, then, didn't He warn us or prevent it from happening?

That is the soul-wrenching struggle with the question of prophecy. What must we know in order to live informed and meaningful lives, while not fully knowing the future?

The Bible says much on this matter. But before I go into specifics, it would be wise to see how the biblical writers handle prophecy. I do so with caution because this is an area where exploitation can be both a temptation and a possibility.

PROPHECY: A TEST FOR AUTHENTICITY

First, the fulfillment or failure of a prophecy is an important test. If a prophecy does not turn out to be true, the Bible makes it clear that the one making the prophecy is a false prophet. There were numerous false prophets in Israel's history, whose goal was to seduce the people into false worship. Power, money, and fear were in varied degrees part of such efforts.

But there were also true prophets whose prophecies were remarkably specific, covering centuries of prediction. Their goal was to keep the people faithful to the one true God, and because their message was not always welcome, their graves are plentiful in the Holy Land. As Jesus said to the people who were trying to manipulate His power for selfish purposes, "You who kill the prophets and stone those sent to you, how often I have longed to gather you" (see Matthew 23:37).

To give us a glimpse of how God has worked in the past, and what that is intended to teach us about both the past and the future—especially for a time such as this—I would like to take a brief look at one prophecy about Babylon.

Babylon (modern day Iraq) is a significant nation in the history of prophecy. In fact, it plays a major part even now in the fulfillment of those very prophecies made centuries ago. In the fifth century before Christ, the ruler of Babylon was Nebuchadnezzar, a pompous, self-aggrandizing despot with designs for world conquest. (Saddam Hussein has said that he sees himself in Nebuchadnezzar's lineage.) Nebuchadnezzar became quite troubled by a recurring dream in which he saw a statue composed of four distinct parts: the head of gold, the chest and arms of silver, the hips and thighs of bronze, and the legs of iron, with the feet partly of iron and partly of clay. The entire episode is described in the Book of Daniel.

In the dream, Nebuchadnezzar watched as this imposing statue was smashed into pieces by a massive stone "uncut by human hands." He was terrified by the vision because he suspected it portended something concerning him (dreams and visions as omens are not uncommon in that culture to this very day). And so, offering a huge reward, he began a nationwide search for someone to interpret it for him. Naturally, there were many takers. But Nebuchadnezzar was not just a man of power. He was also very shrewd. He required the person who claimed he could explain the dream to first describe it. Failure to do so would mean death. Suddenly, there were no offers to interpret the dream.

In the land was a young Jewish man Nebuchadnezzar had brought into captivity. His name was Daniel. Daniel was highly respected as a devout follower of God and was among those considered as a possible interpreter of this dream. Daniel immediately sought God in prayer for an extended time and finally came to the king with the answer. As he began, he made it clear to Nebuchadnezzar that the ability to interpret the dream was not his own, but had been entrusted to him by God. With that proviso, he described the dream with great precision and followed with the interpretation.

The revelation was about four successive empires. Each one, Daniel said, would dominate for a time, but then would be overcome or destroyed by a power greater. Babylon (represented by the gold) would someday be overrun by a conquering neighbor. That nation, in turn, would suffer defeat by a third nation that would a short while later be replaced by yet another ironlike force. Four dominating empires, each displaced by another's megalomaniac designs. The last of the four would break under a power different from any previous earthly regime.

Nebuchadnezzar listened to the interpretation with consternation. We can follow the historic drift and see precisely what happened to Babylon and its successors. The golden days of Nebuchadnezzar's empire came to an end as the Medes and Persians displaced the Babylonians around 538 B.C. They in turn continued until about 330 B.C. when they were overpowered by Greece, which held sway until about 63 B.C. when Greece was finally subdued by Rome.

But of Rome, it was said that it would be destroyed as an empire by "a stone uncut by human hands." What could that description possibly mean? The most common position among Bible scholars is that this describes a power not of human design. The coming of Christ and His return have been seen by most as the boundaryless power, breaking into the consciousness of a people, different from other powers that are typically driven by territorial sovereignty. This explanation makes sense.

For those who would dismiss this extensive prophecy as too general a prediction, in chapter 8, Daniel becomes more specific as to how these empires would fall apart. For example, in his prophecy concerning Greece he describes a young ruler who would become a world conqueror and then would be "suddenly cut off." His rule would be handed over to four different leaders who would gradually blend into two empires and then finally merge into one. Looking back upon history, we see that the life of Alexander the Great was suddenly cut short, and that upon his death his kingdom was indeed divided between four generals. From that era came the Ptolemaic and the Seleucid empires, and then finally, Rome.

All this makes for fascinating reading, and the fact that Christ, "a stone uncut by human hands," changed the world in huge proportions, must give us pause. Though He had no political aspirations (his followers' contrary insistence notwithstanding), two thousand years later we still date our calendars by Him. No nation or empire has captured the conscience of humanity as Jesus has and continues to do.

One might argue that Islam also has a huge following. The difference between the two is profound and real. I recall the response of a man who lived in the midst of a Muslim stronghold when I commented on the seeming national commitment to the religion. His answer was fascinating: "Let [the religious leaders] get their foots off the necks of the people and then see how many continue to follow." That is a challenge that I am afraid Islam will not accept.

In contrast, Christ's rule was not a power framed by kingdom aspirations, but a plea to bring the rule of God into the human heart. That is the key to the Christian life, not world domination through geographical expansion. The Crusades and the politicization of the gospel run counter to the message and method of Jesus Christ, and is a dark blotch upon Christendom. Christianity is a message of a personal relationship with God, albeit a message that has moral implications for one's political perspective. But it never enjoins the control of a people by force in order to propagate the gospel. The power of this truth is moral and rational, never political. Moral force has its own way of conquering, but it is never, by definition, compulsory.

This is so important for understanding the role of prophecy. I see four major areas in which prophecy and supernatural power are at work, even in these recent events. The prediction begins with God and one man.

A PERSON

Three of the world's major religions claim Abraham as their father. Abraham came from Ur, which was part of the Chaldean empire, part of modern day Iraq. He was a wealthy man who sought God with all his heart. He left his home in search of a place that God would assign to him and for which he was willing to leave everything. But as the years went by and he still had no son, he struggled to find a way to ensure he would have an heir. With his wife Sarah's encouragement, Abraham sought to bring a son into the world through Sarah's maidservant, Hagar. Hagar conceived and a son was born, whom they named Ishmael.

Fourteen years after that son was born, Abraham received a vision from God that after all this time, Sarah would conceive. Abraham was amused by this news because of their ages, but the prediction came true. Abraham's wife conceived and a son was born into that household. They named him Isaac. Modern-day Jews trace their ancestry to Isaac, the son of promise, who had a son called Jacob. It was Jacob whose name God changed to Israel. Abraham's older son, Ishmael, was the progenitor of modern day Arabs. The history of the world has been shaped by the struggle between these two brothers, both claiming to be Abraham's legitimate heir.[13]

The Bible leaves no doubt that Isaac is the covenant son and that the land was promised to his descendants. In the Old Testament, God is repeatedly called the God of Abraham, Isaac, and Jacob. Never is

He referred to as the God of Abraham, Ishmael, and Jacob. Is it because He did not love Ishmael? No. It is because Isaac was the covenant son to carry on the promise made to Abraham.

The ensuing contest between Isaac and Ishmael to gain the upper hand, this "jihad" of individual and national proportions, is the story of the Middle East.

The Bible does not hide the blemishes of its heroes. Jacob, the son of Isaac, is shown to be a schemer, a deceiver, and a cheat. He had an extraordinary struggle in following God. By wheeling and dealing he strove to get ahead, only to stumble and make a mess of his personal life. His own brother Esau, whom he had deceived, plotted to kill him. Finally, at the end of his rope, he wrestled with God till God answered his prayer. Though he would carry the physical scar of his struggle the rest of his life, God would bless him. At that moment of divine encounter, when Jacob repented of his efforts to manipulate his destiny, God, in a pure act of grace, forgave him and changed his name to Israel.

Ishmael, on the other hand, having come into the story through Abraham's lack of faith in God's promise of an heir, became an "alien" in his own household. But there was more. He would determine his destiny through power. Even before he was born, God spoke to Hagar, describing the temperament of the young lad and what the future held for him: "He will be a wild donkey of a man; his hand will be against everyone and everyone's hand against him, and he will live in hostility toward all his brothers" (Genesis 16:12).

Is this what we are seeing fulfilled today? Perhaps Abraham was aware of what God had told Hagar about Ishmael's future and struggled with his fear over what might happen in a conflict between the brothers. With God's promise of such miraculous proportion before him, Abraham yet pleaded in prayer that God would not forget Ishmael. God answered him, saying,

> Yes, but your wife Sarah will bear you a son, and you will call him Isaac. I will establish my covenant with him as an everlasting covenant for his descendants after him. And as for Ishmael, I have heard you: I will surely bless him; I will make him fruitful and will greatly increase his numbers. He will be the father of twelve rulers, and I will make him into a great nation. But my covenant I will establish with Isaac, whom Sarah will bear to you by this time next year. (Genesis 17:19–21)

In case you take issue with the Jews being given a privileged role and say, "What else would you expect from the pen of Moses, but to present Isaac as the covenant son?" I suggest you also look at the words of

Muhammad in the Koran:

> And (remember) when Moses said unto his people [the Israelites]: "O my people! Remember Allah's favor unto you, how He placed among you prophets, and He made you kings, and gave you that (which) He gave not to any (other) of (His) creatures. O my people! Go into that holy land which Allah hath ordained for you." (Surah 5:20–21)

Numerous books discuss the intent and extent of all that these texts mean. I just want to draw two lessons from Abraham.

The first is this: Politicians and media pundits can do all they will to anchor our current conflict to this century or the last century. The truth is that this family feud goes back for over four-thousand years as God in His foreknowledge described the temperaments, dispositions, and entailments of this conflict. Virtually every major prophet addresses this issue, including Moses, Isaiah, Jeremiah, Ezekiel, and Daniel. The Bible is established as a prophetic book of great contemporary significance. Events in the Middle East are not taking place in a vacuum. They happen on the basis of a tremendous historical memory.

Second, God's blessing must be received on *His* terms. It must not only be seen in the acquisition of land (or wealth) and power. He did promise a land to this particular people, and He asked in turn for their national allegiance. But through His relationship with the nation of Israel He has incontrovertibly demonstrated over the centuries that even with a clear identity and the best laws of the land, the human heart ever forgets the goodness of God and seeks to build its own future apart from God's blueprint. "Be good and be blessed, be bad and be cursed" is in the end too pragmatic a temptation for us. The reward becomes the goal and ultimately kills genuine goodness, because any attempt to be good apart from God is impossible. Nation building for God will always be vulnerable to the opposition of others who would nation-build without God. The reason, therefore, that democracy makes good government is not because it is perfect, but because it shapes the future with the struggle or the "jihad of ideas," not with the "jihad of the sword." Faith in God and His grace is born of the glad surrender of the heart, not the handcuffed submission of compliance.

Abraham showed the way of faith by being willing even to give up his son, should God have asked that of him, and showing us by his example that God could build a people by faith, independent of national and political forces. Abraham was intended to be a model because of his faith, not because of his wealth or power. To understand today's conflict we must go back to this man's household.

A CITY

It is not just a family or a man of faith that is at the point of contention, but a city, the city of Jerusalem. This historic city is revered by the three great faiths of the world: Judaism, Christianity, and Islam. Islam, of course, denies that the Jews have any right to it at all, while Christians see it as the city for which God had a special love, and the city that would be at the forefront in the end times. Take note, for example, of this extraordinary prophecy in the book of Zechariah written centuries before Jesus Christ.

> This is the word of the LORD concerning Israel. The LORD, who stretches out the heavens, who lays the foundation of the earth, and who forms the spirit of man within him, declares: "I am going to make Jerusalem a cup that sends all the surrounding peoples reeling. Judah will be besieged as well as Jerusalem. On that day, when all the nations of the earth are gathered against her, I will make Jerusalem an immovable rock for all the nations. All who try to move it will injure themselves." (Zechariah 12:1–3)

Here is a prophecy given over twenty-five-hundred

years ago about the city set on a hill that will become, as the King James translation puts it, "a cup of trembling to all who oppose it" (Zechariah 12:2). This city has seen enemies trample her underfoot, her walls built up and destroyed, peace processes stalemated because of her, martyrs dying in her defense, her streets covered with blood, and opposing factions in a titanic struggle calling her home.

Scholars have raised serious questions about the legitimacy or illegitimacy of the Islamic claim that Jerusalem is their holy city. For our purpose, I just point out the specificity of the prophetic voice in reminding us that Jerusalem would be at the center of the conflict. No honest individual can read the Bible and miss the prominent place Jerusalem holds. God Himself said of this city, "See, I have engraved you on the palms of my hands; your walls are ever before me" (Isaiah 49:16). One of the psalmists, while in captivity in Babylon, wrote, "If I forget you, O Jerusalem, may my right hand forget its skill. May my tongue cling to the roof of my mouth if I do not remember you, if I do not consider Jerusalem my highest joy" (Psalm 137:5–6).

Truly, this is a city that cannot be hid and will not be obliterated. It is not accidental that the eternal city is called the New Jerusalem. Ownership of this embattled city has defined success or failure for

Palestinians and Jews alike. That leads us to the next component.

A PEOPLE

The present conflict or tension is not just about a man and his sons, nor is it about a city and its walls. It is about a people and their role in history. If there is any nation that has been given its future, it is the nation of Israel. Four prophecies about the Hebrew people, made long before they were fulfilled, reinforce how accurately the prophets spoke.

First, they would be brought into the Promised Land through a series of miracles. That happened in an extraordinary way under Moses.

Second, because of their moral failure they would be scattered all over the world (see Deuteronomy 28:64; Zechariah 7:14; I Kings 9:6–7). The "wandering Jew" is an epithet based on historic fact.

Third, they would become a byword and a proverb among the nations. Has any group suffered more at the hands of persecutors than the Jewish people? Here, even Christendom has been guilty and bears the shame of having at times been politically motivated to persecute the Jewish race. Thankfully, some within the church have not accepted this misuse of power and have been involved in the rescue of Jewish people. But for centuries we have seen prophecy fulfilled in the persecution of the Jewish people.

Fourth, the Bible speaks of a regathering of the Jewish people from all over the world. Has history ever witnessed anything like the return of Jews to the Promised Land from all over the world, beginning in 1948?

God teaches us lessons of universal proportions in His dealings with Israel. He seeks to win their hearts not because they have any superior merit, but because of His mercy alone. This one people, inheritors of the promise to Abraham, represent to us today the cost, the hazards, and the struggle between following God and abandoning Him. He has shown us that even divinely established law is unable to change the stubbornness of our wills. He has shown us the tendencies of the human heart, not the least of which is our inordinate ability to go against reason, common sense, and even miracle. He has shown that grace misunderstood will invariably breed jealousy between even the closest of relationships. No one can bear the success of another unless every enablement is viewed as the mercy of God demonstrated in different ways. He has shown the folly of thinking that we can accelerate the march of history on our own terms. He has shown us that politics is one of the most fragile of all institutions, empowering goodness but susceptible to great abuse. He has shown us that politicizing morality and religion is deadly when it becomes a means of control rather than an expression of the true, the good, and the beautiful. He has shown that in the end we will prove that though His way may seem narrow, it is actually the broadest of all freedoms, and that our way, which may seem wide, is the narrowest of all bigotries. He has shown us that people matter more than systems, and if a system exploits people, the system is corrupt. He has shown us that sometimes He can use "less righteous" people as an instrument to awaken those who have taken their spiritual strength and material blessing for granted. He has shown us that true faith is not controlled by the sword, but by the surrender of the will to the grace and the mercy of God. He has shown us that He can make or break a nation, with or without human agency, and do so in a moment. He has shown us, as the psalmist said, that, "His pleasure is not in the strength of the horse, nor his delight in the legs of a man; the LORD delights in those who fear him, who put their hope in his unfailing love" (Psalm 147:10). He has shown us that to whom much is given, much is also required. He has shown us that ultimately history is His story written upon humanity. And the centerpiece of His story is given to us also in prophecy.

That leads us to the fifth component.

A SON

Zechariah, a prophet during the early fifth century before Christ, speaks more of the Messiah than any other prophet, with the exception of Isaiah. Listen to what he says in the same chapter in which he talks about Jerusalem being a cup of trembling. Writing about the closing days of history and the nation of Israel, he says,

> And I will pour out on the house of David and the inhabitants of Jerusalem a spirit of grace and supplication. They will look on me, the one they have pierced, and they will mourn for him as one mourns for an only child, and grieve bitterly for him as one grieves for a firstborn son. (Zechariah 12:10)

Need one say much more than this? What began with a man, and continued through a family, a nation, and the whole world, culminates in a glimpse of one crucified.

Before Jesus was born in Bethlehem, the prophet Isaiah had said

> *For to us a child is born,*
> *to us a son is given,*
> *and the government will be on his shoulders.*
>
> *And he will be called*
> *Wonderful Counselor, Mighty God,*
> *Everlasting Father, Prince of Peace.*

*Of the increase of his government and peace
there will be no end.*

(ISAIAH 9:6−7)

You see, only the child was born. The Son was not
born; the Son was given. He was not born because He
eternally exists. His name is Jesus. He is the stone
uncut by human hands. He came to offer forgiveness
to us all and to teach us what it means to be part of
His family and to honor one another. Humility was
His hallmark. Goodness was His essence. When Peter
tried to keep Him from being arrested, He told Peter
to put away his sword. In His life, in His death, and in
His resurrection, He showed us what a perfect life
looks like. He built no earthly kingdom and refused to
be conscripted as a king, but He raised up a
formidable group of followers who, with His message,
have conquered the hearts of men and women
throughout history. He sought no political power
because control is not the same thing as reverence. He
told us to set our eyes not upon bricks and mortar, but
upon a city whose builder and maker is God. He seeks
to dwell not in buildings made with hands, but in the
hearts of men and women. The Christian faith is not
about land or a place. It is about a relationship.

Augustine said of Rome that it loved Romulus and

therefore made him a god. By contrast, Jesus was understood to be God and was therefore loved. Even Napoleon conceded that Jesus' way of conquering would outlast the method of those who conquered by the sword. How differently Jesus works from any human agency. The difficult struggle for us is to find the balance between our legitimate patriotic love and the equally legitimate realization that one day all the cities of men will fall to the ground. Augustine wept when he heard that barbarians had scaled Rome's walls. Then he picked up his pen and wrote his famed *City of God.*

A PROPHECY BEYOND ETHNICITY

Abraham sought a city or kingdom whose builder and maker is God. Unfortunately, as he tried in his own wisdom to engineer the future, a world of terror was unleashed from a single family—his own. But he also left as his legacy an example of what it means to live by faith and the difference that makes.

The ultimate city is the eternal one, and when the Apostle John saw a glimpse of that future dwelling, this is the way he described it:

> I looked and there before me was a great
> multitude that no one could count, from every

nation, tribe, people and language, standing before the throne and in front of the Lamb.... They fell down on their faces before the throne and worshiped God, saying:

"Amen!
Praise and glory
and wisdom and thanks and honor
and power and strength
be to our God for ever and ever.
Amen!"

(REVELATION 7:9–12)

That picture portrays what the gospel message is all about. The Lamb of God was Jesus Christ offered up as a sacrifice so that we might draw near by faith because of His gift of life. That offer is made not to people of one language or one race, but to the whole world. Yes, Jews, Arabs, Afghans, Indians, Europeans, and Americans will be there. Every nation, tongue, and tribe is represented in that magnificent vision.

The bin Ladens of this world, who seek earthly kingdoms and who hate others because of their national identity, speak a different language from that of God's Word. From a cave in Afghanistan, this murderer conceived the death and destruction of several thousand people. He had no knowledge of who would die and who would live. He just sought to destroy a symbol of something he despised—America and the freedom she represents.

But those who struggle in their own wisdom to find the way to God will find out that the ultimate struggle took place on a cross two thousand years ago. From that cross comes a different message and a different kingdom. It is a kingdom of love and truth; and it is ultimately personal, not national. The message of Jesus is a message of forgiveness and peace that the world cannot give or take away. He looks beyond our race, our skills, our strengths, and our attainments. He looks into our hearts and sees our needs.

He knows the beginning from the end, yet He will do nothing to destroy our freedom. He gives it to us as a most precious gift. He gives us enough information about the future to know that He is in control, but denies us comprehensive knowledge so that love is never predetermined; it must be freely chosen. That is why the Scriptures often say, "He that has ears to hear let him hear." Our faith is not national but personal, and that is the way it is meant to be.

HEALING THE HURT

I heard a parable years ago as a child growing up in India. It was somewhat rough and unpleasant, but it carried a profound message. A man in one village loved a woman in another village. One day she said to him, "If you really want my love, you will have to prove to me that you love me more than anyone else." He assured her that this was already the case. "Oh no," she said, "you love your mother more than you love me." As the dialogue went back and forth, he asked her what it would take to prove to her that he loved her more than anyone else. "Bring me your mother's heart in your hand," she insisted.

In anguish, the man wrestled with her demand and his love for his mother. In a frenzied moment, wanting desperately to win her, he killed his mother. Wrenching her heart out of her body, he clasped it against him and began to run across the miles to give it to the woman whose love he wanted.

But as he ran through a section of the woods, he stumbled and fell. The heart flew out of his hands, and when he got up, he could not find it. He searched frantically on the ground until he finally found it. As he stood and brushed the dirt from his hands and knees, suddenly he heard a quiet voice coming from the heart, "Son, are you hurt? Son, are you hurt?"

The Mohammed Attas and bin Ladens of our world entice young men into causes of hate and malice. They beckon them to ruthlessly murder people and present their victims to God in order to win His approval. But in doing so, they are really telling us about their own intoxication with pride and devilish addiction to power. They frame the world in their own image; a world of smoldering ruins.

From the cross of Jesus Christ comes a different message. Through the rubble of human antagonism and hate and cruelty, we look upon Him whom we have all pierced because we did not want His way of peace, and we hear His quiet voice asking us, "Are you hurt? Are you hurt?"

Yes, we hurt. We are hurting deeply.

Healing can begin when we receive forgiveness and pursue the future God's way, not ours. The way to life is through the Cross, and the Cross alone. There, hearts are changed one at a time, and life and peace replace death and hate. Those who seek life His way find it. Those who seek it their way lose it. In that sense we can know the future.

> I said to the man at the Gate of the Year, "Give me a light that I may walk safely into the unknown."
>
> He said to me, "Go out into the darkness, and put your hand into the hand of God, and it shall be to you better than the light, and safer than the known."
>
> — KING GEORGE VI

CHAPTER FIVE

WAS GOD PRESENT
or ABSENT?

Every thinking person has at some time raised the question, "Where is God in the midst of suffering?" That question without doubt echoed in millions of minds on September 11, and continues to do so. If illustration were argument, an event such as this would give fodder to both sides of the issue—to those who want to establish the complete absence of God and to those who testify that He exists and is involved in the circumstances of our lives. To a watching world, the finest testimonials to the faith of the nation were the crowded churches the following Sunday and the extraordinary national memorial service. President Bush himself planned the service and led the nation to seek the comfort of God in that time of crisis.

Stepping back from the scene, two starkly different stories from September 11 represent the struggle of the search for God. One story was told by the men of

Ladder 6, a company of the New York City Fire Department. Seven firemen were helping a sixty-nine-year-old woman by the name of Josephine down from the seventy-third floor of one of the World Trade Center towers. These brave men, already laboring under 110 pounds of equipment on their backs, led Josephine step by step down the staircase. At times, she was ready to give up, but they helped, encouraged, inspired, and assured her she would make it. "They were like angels to me," she said. She would stop to catch her breath and they would stop with her. She started to shiver with fear and one gave her his jacket. One floor at a time they got her down until, finally, she could walk no more and just sat down on one of the steps of the fourth floor.

They waited with her, coaxing her to stand up and resume walking because they were almost to the ground floor. But she could not move, and they refused to leave her. Suddenly, they heard and felt the floors beneath them give way under the tremendous weight of the collapsing building, and they were hurtled down with terrific force and enveloped in a suffocating cloud of pitch-black smoke. One of them even prayed, "God, if this is it, please let it be quick."

But as the noise lessened and the smoke began to clear, they found that they had settled over the rubble of the caved-in floors below them. Miraculously,

Josephine had refused to go any farther at the one point that remained intact as the building fell. All seven firemen plus Josephine were eventually brought into the daylight of safety.

"Had we continued descending when we were pleading with her to keep moving," they said, "we would have been killed by the crush of the floors above us." One of them added, "Josephine was like an angel sent from God to stop us so that we could be safe."

How can we react to a story such as this but to concede that those who were rescued in this way saw the hand of God leading, guiding, and stopping their steps?

Yet, not every story ended like Josephine's. The hearts of thousands of others who lost loved ones may well throb with a different emotion. I think of one young woman who, through weeks of struggle, torn by indecision at the marriage proposal of a young man, finally made her choice during the night. In the pre-dawn hours of the 11th she phoned his office at the World Trade Center from her home in California. Her message awaited him when he arrived at work, with words of love and the welcome news that she would marry him. But at midmorning when she retrieved her own messages, her world was unforgettably changed. The voice she heard was not the voice of a man exultant at the news of her acceptance. Instead, she listened to the terror in his voice as he told her that he loved her with all his heart, but his building had been struck by an airplane and was beginning to crumble before his eyes. No angels dragged him to safety.

Was God near or far? Any time a catastrophic event happens, numerous human-interest stories give God glory, while others give Him blame.

THE PROBLEM IS GREATER THAN WE THINK

Theologians have an interesting description for this predicament. They call it "the hiddenness of God," or "divine hiding." Why does God not make His presence more obvious? Many arguments are offered for why God "hides" in a world that seeks to see Him.

The answer is ultimately found in the divine purposes of God. It is not that God has absconded or is absent; it is that there is a divine purpose behind His visibility or invisibility. If one can rightly read the clues, the mystery is opened up in profound ways. Just as evil can be understood only in the light of the ultimate purpose, so also must God's presence or seeming absence be judged on the basis of His purpose.

Certainly, antagonists do not hold their fire on this issue. Yale philosopher Norwood Russell Hanson criticizes God's absence in this way:

> Suppose that on next Tuesday morning, just after breakfast, all of us in this one world are knocked to our knees by a percussive and ear shattering thunderclap. Snow swirls; Leaves drop from trees; The earth heaves and buckles; Buildings topple and towers tumble; The sky is ablaze with an eerie, silvery light. Just then, as all the people of this world look up, the heavens open—The clouds pull apart—Revealing an unbelievably immense and radiant Zeus-like figure, towering above us like a hundred Everests. He frowns darkly as lightning plays across the features of His Michelangeloid face. He then points down at me and exclaims, for every man, woman and child to hear, "I have had quite enough of your too-clever logic-chopping and word-watching in matters of Theology. Be assured, N. R. Hanson, that I do most certainly exist.[14]

Just to assure us that he was not kidding, Hanson adds, "Please do not dismiss this example as a playful, irreverent Disney-oid contrivance. The conceptual point here is that if such a remarkable event were to transpire, I for one should certainly be convinced that God does exist."

I can't blame Hanson for representing his case in such melodramatic terms. I too would love for God to make some indisputable appearance; a rending of the skies with a sound and light accompaniment. But I am not at all sure that believability is as simple as that. So, I have a question for this professor: Suppose this actually happened, exactly the way you asked for it. Would you be satisfied with that epiphany if, moments later while backing out of your driveway, you accidentally ran over your five-year-old son? What would you want from God then? Would you be content with the vision of God that you had experienced a few minutes before, or would you demand an explanation for this tragedy, as well?

Sporadic supernatural demonstrations by God would not satisfy our insistence that He be constantly accountable to us for His actions. The demand that we place before Him—that just one incontrovertible miracle would dispel all doubt in every other case of "divine hiding"—may well be another intellectual smoke screen we hide behind.

That expectation that we put upon God tells us more about ourselves than it does about God. It is ironic, is it not, that Hanson asks for some kind of thunderous event with God in the skies, and yet he is probably among those who dismiss as a chance event the Big Bang of the beginnings of the world? No thoughts of God's involvement there are entertained.

Numerous times in the Scriptures, signs were asked from God, and they were given. But in spite of that, trust in God was not automatic. Probably no disciple received more displays of God's power than the apostle Peter. He was one of only three who witnessed the Transfiguration of Jesus. Jesus had taken His disciples to the top of a mountain where they saw a sight not given to any other human eye. They saw Jesus' body begin to glow with a whiteness that was almost blinding. Suddenly, Moses and Elijah appeared and began to talk with Jesus. Peter asked Jesus if he could build shelters there for the three luminaries, but a voice thundered from the heavens saying, "This is my Son. Listen to Him" (see Luke 9:35). This experience had everything—Sight! Sound! Words! Power! Peter was so overcome that he did not want to go down from the mountain. But Jesus told them it was time to return to the humdrum world of their day-to-day existence.

Jesus was not playing games with his disciples; giving them a glimpse of the eternal and then taking it away from them. Rather, He was showing them the greater reality from which He came and to which He will take us, without denying the present reality through which He works in us. Both are important. We cannot escape the struggle of day-to-day thinking and doing and being by some sort of spellbinding incident that suddenly invades our circumstances. Life is to be lived at a level where the norm becomes meaningful in the light of eternal values, rather than interpreting eternal values according to what is normal for us. That is key to understanding our yearning for the future and our struggle with the present.

But there is more. Jesus was trying to help His disciples to understand the frailty He saw in them—their chronic bent to be enchanted every moment. Peter saw the proof of Jesus' divinity in His transfiguration. He did not doubt after that who Jesus was. Yet, when Jesus was arrested, Peter floundered and even denied that he ever knew Jesus. He was in momentary awe of the miraculous but could not trust God for the future. This failing was also common in Israel's exodus from Egypt. The people would witness a miracle and follow God with national repentance. But as soon as God seemed to hide for some time, the grumbling and skepticism began.

The examples of Israel and of Peter are repeated endlessly in our own experiences. We have a limitless ability to trust God only when it suits our purpose. Rather than allowing God to be God and serving Him for who He is, *we* actually try to play God and *He* becomes our subject, expected to do our bidding at our every whim. I do not know of any greater fickleness in the human heart than this. We lie to ourselves after a miraculous event, believing it will have staying power. But the moment another steep hill appears before us, we wonder whether the miracle we witnessed some time back actually happened or was only a delusion. Reality is threatened by this fickleness, and if we do not understand and accept this, we live in an illusionary world of chronic skepticism. Our demand for more information is, in a real sense, a fight against our finitude.

THE SOLUTION MUST GO DEEPER THAN WE SEEK

A subtle delusion keeps us from the real battle. The truth behind our clamor for explanation is that we assume ourselves to be only intellectual entities and thus, if only our intellect can be satisfied, we will be content. This mangling of our personalities lies at the root of our disconnectedness from the way God has framed reality.

One of the most powerful encounters in the Bible is between Jesus and a learned man named Nicodemus. Nicodemus recognized the supernatural character of Jesus and said to Him, "Teacher, no one could do the miracles you are doing unless God is with him" (see John 3:2). That tacit endorsement could have easily elicited a commendation from Jesus. Instead, Jesus challenged Nicodemus that if he wanted to be part of God's kingdom, he needed to have a new birth. This was not the direction Nicodemus had planned on going, but Jesus knew exactly what He was about. He was telling Nicodemus that it is not the miracle over matter that ultimately has staying power; it is the miracle over the way we think about reality that has eternal ramifications. We are not all intellect, and therefore some need beyond the intellect needs to be met.

But there is a second point I wish to make. We look for God to be something concrete, something we can see or handle or fully explain. This is a fallacy born out of our addiction to the external, and human history has repeatedly challenged that disposition. There are many evidences of God's miracle-working presence. Incredible stories abound for which there is often no natural interpretation that satisfactorily explains them.

The supernatural is possible. It happens, but it does not lead to the greatest miracle in a life. For you see, anyone can take a miraculous story and explain it a dozen different ways. At best it just proves that there is a power beyond our own. So where does that leave us? What God seeks in every individual is not just companionship based on His intervention, but communion with Him based on His indwelling. That is what makes the difference when a building is collapsing. It is not whether a hand grabs your hand

and rescues you from the carnage; it is that no matter what happens, His strength empowers you to rise beyond the devastation.

If mankind were only mind or intellect, evidence from the physical world would be all that mattered. But there is a depth to our being, a spiritual essence that goes deeper than our intellect. That essence hungers for intimacy. If you will pardon the crassness of the analogy, "making love," as popular jargon describes sexual consummation without deep commitment, is no more love than the embrace of a pickpocket signifies affection. The spiritual not the physical is the essence of our being, and for that quality of nearness, only communion with the living God satisfies. We are spiritual beings and God responds to us in spirit.

The reason this kind of communion is needed is well articulated by the scientist and mystic, Blaise Pascal. He argued that if there were no obscurity to God, humanity would not feel its corruption, and if there were no light to bring Him near, humanity could not hope for a cure. That thought, coming from the father of the modern-day computer, is even more significant. He knew that though empirical truth is good, it is not good enough. He longed for the mystery and the intimacy of God, something mere intellect could not deliver.

What is the difference between companionship and communion? In companionship with God we come to Him, recognizing our limit of strength. In communion with God we stay with Him, recognizing our depth of spirit. In companionship with God we long to see and understand. In communion with God we long to feel and belong. Those who seek companionship without communion seek power without commitment, a display without dedication, and proof without love.

This truth eludes our pragmatic bent and reconstructs many of the realities God intended for us to live with. English spiritual writer Anthony Bloom underscored this ailment of ours well:

> We complain that God does not make Himself present to us for the few minutes we reserve for Him, but what about the 23 hours during which God may be knocking at our door and we answer, "I am busy. I am sorry"? Or when we do not answer at all because we do not even hear the knock at the door of our heart, of our mind, of our conscience, of our life. So there is a situation in which we have no right to complain of the absence of God, because we are a great deal more absent than He ever is.[15]

But this is where we break free from the entanglements and distractions to find the hand of

God. *Communion with God takes place in our solitariness before it takes effect in community.* Henri Nouwen captured this profound truth: "In solitude we can unmask the illusion of our possessiveness and discern in the center of our own self that we are not what we can conquer, but what is given to us. Through that solitude He leads us to communion."[16] In other words, it is not our victories that make us who we are; it is His divine presence that carries us through both victory and defeat, and defines us.

Is this possibly what C. S. Lewis had in mind in *The Voyage of the Dawn Treader?* Lucy has been desperately seeking the presence of Aslan when suddenly He appears before her. "Oh Aslan," she says, "It was kind of you to come."

"I have been here all the time," said He, "but you have just made me visible."

"Aslan," said Lucy, almost a little reproachfully. "Don't make fun of me. As if anything I could do would make you visible!"

"It did," said Aslan. "Do you think I wouldn't obey my own rules?"

What are His rules? "You will seek me and find me when you seek me with all your heart" (Jeremiah 29:13).

I would not at all be surprised to learn someday, when the words and thoughts of those who died in the devastation of September 11 are revealed in God's presence, that many, many of them knew a profound sense of His presence, even when they knew life in its earthly sojourn was coming to an end.

THERE ARE APPOINTMENTS FROM WHICH WE CANNOT RUN

There is at least one profound lesson that I draw from the life and death stories of September 11. There is an appointed time for each of us when life will meet its end. God has entrusted us with common sense and wisdom that we must express in our day-to-day activities. We are not to throw life away. We are not licensed to court danger. But sometimes we can think that we are safe when we are not. Real safety is only to be found in His presence. Wherever we go, whatever we do, we are safe in that communion with Him. Safety is not found in seeking an escape from His appointments.

One-time chaplain to the United States Senate, Peter Marshall, told a story, called "Rendezvous in Samara," of a man who worked as the servant of a wealthy merchant. He had gone into town to shop for the day when suddenly he felt someone brush heavily against his shoulder. Somewhat offended, he turned toward the person who had jostled him, and found himself staring into a pair of eyes that spoke death to him. Panicking, he dropped everything and ran home. His master saw him running breathlessly toward the house and met him on the front steps.

"What on earth is the matter?" asked the master.

"Oh, sir! Someone in the marketplace rudely brushed me, and when I turned to face him, he looked like the Angel of Death to me. He too had a look of shock on his face. It was almost as if he wanted to grab me but then backed away. I am afraid, sir. I don't want to go back to the market."

"Saddle one of our horses and ride all day till you reach the distant village of Samara," the master said. "Stay there till you get word from me that it is safe for you to return."

The servant rode off, and the master made his way to the market to find the person who had so frightened his servant. As he wound his way through the crowded streets, he suddenly came face to face with this strange looking individual.

"Who are you?" the merchant said. "Are you the one who just scared my servant?"

"Yes, indeed."

"Why did you frighten him?"

"Well, I was truly surprised to see him here. I am the Angel of Death, and I chose to spend the day here before heading to my stop for tonight. You see, it was not so much that I surprised him, as that he surprised me. I did not expect to see him here because I have an appointment with him in Samara tonight."

That is the reality we all live with. Death is the moment we all seek to flee, yet it is a moment that the Bible says has been set for each of us before it ever comes to be. King David said it this way,

> *For you created my inmost being;*
> *you knit me together in my mother's womb.*

> *All the days ordained for me*
> *were written in your book before*
> *one of them came to be.*
> (PSALM 139:13,16)

We must learn to live every day to the fullest, in healthy recognition that one day it will be the last. Was it not ironic that one of the passengers who died in the American Airlines crash in Queens, New York, in early November 2001 had escaped the inferno of the World Trade Center tragedy in September? Another passenger on that plane was a young sailor who had just returned from extended duty overseas on the USS *Enterprise.*

We can flee the marketplace, only to find that the quiet village of Samara is where our rendezvous was to be.

There Is a Friendship in Which We Cannot Lose

The Bible tells of the time when Lazarus, one of Jesus' friends, took ill. His family sent word for Jesus to come and heal him, but by the time Jesus came, Lazarus was dead. His sisters greeted Jesus with the sharp words, "If you had been here, our brother would not have died" (see John 11:21). Jesus went to the tomb and wept. But as He dried His tears, He performed the remarkable miracle of raising Lazarus from the dead.

But if Jesus knew He was going to do this, why did He weep before the tomb? I suggest that He wept because He knew that someday, even with this momentary reprieve, Lazarus would come to his "Samara," and the pain of death would once again be very real.

Jesus' miracle was to remind them that "Samara" was not the end. He said to the family gathered, "I am the resurrection and the life. He who believes in me will live, even though he dies" (see John 11:25). His miracle is not to be there to keep us from dying. It is to take us through death into His eternal presence, which is the place of ultimate communion.

Some years ago, I was in Israel and visited the village of Bethany where Lazarus's body once lay before Jesus raised him. A few months ago, I stood by the tomb of Lazarus in Larnaca, Cyprus, where he had become the bishop of the church. That tomb was excavated nearly one thousand years ago, and the simple inscription on the grave said, "Lazarus, Bishop of Larnaca—Four days dead, Friend of Jesus."

The first tomb reminded me of the possibility of the miracle; the second, of the reality of death. The inscription spoke of the greatest miracle and reality of all—communion with the living God. That intimate friendship is the kind of communion that helps you face death knowing that your Friend is with you beyond the grave.

Even the Koran recognizes that Jesus had the power to raise the dead; a power that it does not attribute to Muhammad. That same power was in the World Trade Center on September 11. Bin Laden and his band of murderers may have had the power to kill, but Jesus Christ has the power to raise us up again. That is what communion with Him brings. His presence is within us, and terrorists can never take that away.

CHAPTER SIX

WHERE DO WE GO *from* HERE?

The dark shadow cast by the attacks on September 11 has not been without a glimmer of light. Yes, the lives that were lost will never be recovered, and for many families, life has been unalterably changed. But picking up the pieces and facing life anew is not only a grim reality; it is a necessary step forward. Pain will always scar the memory, but hope and strength can harness it for good. We would do well to remember that in some parts of the world the destruction of human life is so common that numerous atrocities go unreported. This daring attack on the United States, however, with the world as its audience, was one of historic proportion. When President Bush said that uprooting terrorism would become the focus of his presidency, he put this challenge in legitimate perspective. He has not overstated its importance.

A few months prior to September 11, my wife and I had the opportunity to speak with the president. We told him that we had prayed for him throughout the presidential elections and the unbelievable circumstances that kept the decision in doubt, and he said to us, "That was a cliffhanger, wasn't it? But you know," he added, "I believe that God must have placed me here for a purpose." I have to believe that God did indeed position this highly focused and gifted man for a task such as this—to lead the world through this time of incredible crisis.

By the grace of God, America has the leadership, the military strength, the courage, and the will to respond. But we will need to give careful thought to the following four areas if we are to face the immense possibilities and threats of the future.

GOD AND CULTURE

The inability to think critically and logically or to draw a distinction between worldviews is a casualty of our time. We will never come to the truth on serious matters of faith and belief if we do not know how to think our way through those beliefs. Through this event religion has come to the fore, but much that has been said about it has not been positive. Many in the media, such as the noted journalist Andrew Sullivan, have used the opportunity to focus on the destruction religion can bring.[17] Sullivan is a brilliant writer, one of the more readable journalists of our day, but he is tragically misguided in his discussion of this issue. I do not know the motivation behind some of his sweeping and sometimes condescending statements, but his method that combines truth with error is dangerous and must be addressed.

To view all religion in the same light and stigmatize beliefs with broad and equivocating statements, necessitates a serious castigation of the truth. Sullivan's article generalizes the dangers of religion and refers to Christian "right-wing fundamentalists" in the same terms as thugs at the beck and call of bin Laden. (It is true, by the way, that in the past century more people were killed under the banner of irreligion than by religious fanatics.) He comes dangerously close to caricaturing true faith, denuding all faiths of their essence, and then granting them limited freedoms as a courtesy. While denying absolutes, he introduces his own thoroughly secular absolutes on the subject of religion. This is clever but irresponsible journalism. One would expect more from a man of Sullivan's stature and ability than this tendentious treatment of a difficult subject.[18]

It is pivotal that people learn to sift out the difference between good reasoning and a philosophical prejudice that selectively undermines whole systems of thought. Let me point out one major failure in Sullivan's logic.

A simple law in logic is called the Undistributed Middle. It means that just because two things have one thing in common, doesn't mean they have everything in common. An example of this kind of reasoning is that since elephants have ears and I have ears, I must be an elephant.

To undermine the role of religion in society because some religious extremists take advantage of their religious privilege, is no more legitimate than to say that freedom of the press causes the murder of innocent people and should therefore be curtailed: For had not the press telecast the demonstrations that took place at Tiananmen Square against human rights violations in China, the Chinese authorities would never have been able to identify key figures and single them out for retribution. Therefore, according to this logic, members of the press, including Mr. Sullivan, should have some of their freedoms restricted. By his reasoning we would have to condemn all politics because of Timothy McVeigh's skewed politics. We would have to be wary of the Mahatma Gandhis and the Martin Luther Kings because of radicals in the peace movements.

Differentiating between moral viewpoints is imperative for the American culture, even if some of those perspectives are religious ones. For America this is a moment of decision. In the eighteenth century, Alexis de Tocqueville said that America is great because it is good; if it ever ceases to be good, it will cease to be great. He recognized that America's spiritual bent was at the heart of her moral thinking. If we change what is at the root of who we are by marginalizing the public expression of religious thought, we place our future at enormous risk.

Culture and Country

It is time for those of us who have come to this wonderful land to make some uncompromising decisions. Yes, the cultures we bring with us are precious to us, but they cannot override the legitimate expectation of loyalty to this nation and a commitment to its safety and well-being. If our loyalty to America is threatened by allegiance to the culture or heritage of our upbringing, as wonderful as that culture may be, America is placed at tremendous risk.

In a pluralistic society there will always be a struggle to find shared values. But if those shared values are made secondary to a radically different set of values that, at heart, undermine our national freedoms, America will become purely a means to an end that could be in violation of its own reason for being. (It is interesting to note how difficult Islamic countries make it for those of other faiths living among them, but how demanding Islam can be of the American culture to provide it unlimited freedom.) One is entitled to freedom, but one is not free from the responsibility to protect the nation's right to exist on the terms that made it great in the first place. Culture is dangerous when it is used to hijack the basic ethos of a nation. If that ethos is not respected, the very strengths that made the country attractive to the immigrant in the first place are abused.

I came to this country because I admired its freedoms. I cherish the opportunities that have been given to me here to excel and to be what God has called me to be. I owe this land my allegiance and I love its people. It is time to ask the hard question of ourselves: If we do not love this country, why are we here? Neutrality is an illusion.

COUNTRY AND HISTORY

We must find ways to remember what happened on September 11 without becoming preoccupied by it and without building into our children a martyr complex. September 11 must be put into the context of the many great tragedies and losses of life that humanity has faced across history. If we allow our perspective to become too narrow, we face the danger of misrepresenting this dreadful act as something that is dreadful only because it happened to us. Many nations before us have lived through terror. Wicked people will always be looking for the opportunity to carry out their evil goals. It is the duty of the good to be willing to pay with their lives so that the light of truth may continue to be upheld against the lies of wickedness. This universally felt tragedy must be memorialized in our hearts, so that we remain vigilant and determined to resist the scourge of violence. But we must not forget that we are not alone in our experience and in our pain. We are hurting now because we are going through the same dark valley that others have traveled before, and where still others will be in the future. We must realize the strength that comes from shared experience.

In the aftermath of this tragedy, I have often thought back to the song, "The Massacre of Glencoe." This song, with its haunting melody, has kept alive the memory of the terrible slaughter that took place in Glencoe, Scotland, on 13 February 1692. To this day a lone piper walks daily through the mists of that now serene valley, reminding the people of an event centuries before. The words of the song tell the story.

Oh cruel is the snow that sweeps Glencoe,
and covers the graves o'Donald.
Oh cruel was the foe that raped Glencoe,
and murdered the house of MacDonald.

They came in a blizzard, we offered them heat,
a roof o'er their heads, dry shoes for their feet,
we wined them and dined them, they ate of our meat,
and they slept in the house of MacDonald.

They came from Fort William with murder in mind,
the Campbells had orders, King William had signed,
put all to the sword, these words underlined,
leave no one alive called MacDonald.

They came in the night while our men were asleep,
this band of Argylls, through snow soft and deep,
like murdering foxes among helpless sheep,
they butchered the house of MacDonald.

Some died in their beds at the hand of the foe,
some fled in the night and were lost in the snow,
some lived to accuse him, who struck the first blow,
but gone was the house of MacDonald.[19]

Every time I hear that song, I think of how horrific that night must have been. In terms of the actual loss of life, worse events took place in Scottish history. The betrayal of friendship is what makes the horror of this event so unforgettable. We can now relate. The eerie, vacant spot in New York City's skyline is a grim reminder of what has happened to us at the hands of those to whom we opened our borders as friends, but who came to destroy us. How well we remember this will help the next generation keep watch.

HISTORY AND HIS STORY

To save people at one's own risk is a God-like act. We were moved to tears as we watched how carefully and tirelessly the rescue workers labored to find anyone who may have survived this tragedy. Those are the pictures we will carry the rest of our lives—faces covered with soot and dirt, workers laboring night and day till the last one is rescued.

Jesus tells a parable of a shepherd who left his ninety-nine sheep safely in the fold in order to look for the one that was missing. This little story is instructive in more ways than meet the eye, for it becomes apparent that it is not just that the individual is important, but that the one who is doing the searching is God Himself.

I think back to the story of Genelle Guzman at the beginning of this book. As she clawed and scratched at the debris, desperate that someone hear her, her hope was realized because someone had put aside his own comfort and safety in order to find her. This simple truth is a metaphor of the Gospel of Jesus Christ.

Numerous times we are reminded in the Gospel that He is in search of us, that He came to seek and to save those who are lost. This truth puts everything into perspective for us. We think we are looking for Him. We find out that *He* has come searching for *us.* We think we have been searching for God, wondering where He was in the misery unleashed by wicked men on September 11. Someday we may find out that the real story was that God was reaching out to us, trying to show us what is in our own hearts and reminding us of who we are.

The dastardly acts of September 11 were schemed in the caves of Afghanistan. In a cave two thousand years ago, God sent us His answer. His reaching for us, and His longing for us, took shape in the person of His Son, Jesus. And the light of His love continues to reach across time and distance to each one of us, exactly where we are.

The famed trapeze artist Rodleigh gives me a glimpse of what goes on between the one suspended in air, hurtling through space, and the one waiting for the right split second to grab him and keep him from falling: "When I fly to Joe I have simply to stretch out my arms and hands and wait for him to catch me and pull me safely over the apron behind the catchbar.... You see, the worst thing a flyer can do is to try to catch the catcher.... Don't try to grab him; he will grab you. Just stretch out your arms and hands and trust, trust, trust."[20]

If you do not know the grip of God's hand on you, as you hang between hope and cynicism, He has a promise for you. God, through the prophet Isaiah, said:

> *"So do not fear, for I am with you;*
> *do not be dismayed, for I am your God.*
> *I will strengthen you and help you;*
> *I will uphold you with my righteous right hand."*
>
> (ISAIAH 41:10)

This is the same God whose hands were pierced for you so that He could reach you with the light of His love. When safely in His grip, you too will breathe a sigh of gratitude and say, "Thank God. The struggle is over."

This may be America's moment. We as a nation—and every individual in search of the truth—will find security in the rubble of our lives only as we place ourselves in His hands. And we will find a way out of the confusion of the debris of life only because He is the light.

STEADYING *the* SOUL WHILE *the* HEART IS BREAKING

September 11, 2001: A day when millions of hearts were broken, if not shattered. Who of us will ever forget it? I was in Bangkok when the carnage took place. A few days later, as I boarded a plane in Paris to return home, the silence aboard the aircraft spoke volumes. The flight attendants and pilots represented an industry plundered and abused by lawless men for the slaughter of innocent people. They had colleagues who were used as ammunition to desecrate and murder. Behind me sat a couple whose son-in-law had been killed in the Pentagon attack. Their daughter is left expecting their first child, who will now be fatherless. A Belgian businessman sat next to me in as much of a state of shock as I was. He worked for the International Monetary Fund and well knew that money alone would never be the solution to this carnage.

Upon arrival at my hotel in Washington, the Pakistani taxi driver who took me said in Hindi, "They trampled our hearts under their feet and then smashed them with their hands...their consciences have rotted."

The immigration officer in Washington looked at my passport, showing dozens of countries visited, and then reached out his hand and said, "Welcome home, Mr. Zacharias."

That journey summed it up. With those who hurt with you, there was something in common. With the murderers and those who applaud them, we have no common value. That lies at the heart of this tragedy. The fact is, in a tragedy as complex as this, there are several converging issues. I raise four of them.

The first is cultural. Any time you seek to find a solution of conscience there must be some common ground—a common value and an ultimate rule by which we judge our conduct. With the killers of September 11 the civilized world has no common ground. They are creatures of hate whose anger could never be satisfied except by building a cloud of hell over humanity. I remember a Middle Eastern leader's answer years ago when asked, "When will the terrorists' killing stop in your part of the world?"

"When they love their children more than they hate us," came the reply. Such is the problem with the suicide squads unleashed upon America. Their irreverent lives victimize even their own families, their own countrymen, and indeed, their own faith.

I think it is time to ask some honest and painful questions of those of all cultures that seek a home in America. Do we love this country? Is our allegiance to this land where we, as strangers, have come because of some shared values? As long as the answer is qualified by some other ethnic or cultural contingency, however noble that may sound, we will never serve this land with our hearts. We will do so only for our pocketbooks. This is one of the most hospitable nations in the world. Are we here to share in its goodness or rape and abuse its kindness?

I have traveled around the world numerous times. I have cast my life and lot here because there is no other place I would rather live. This is now my home and its people are my fellow-countrymen and women. When the immigration officer welcomed me "home," I was too tearfilled to get even one word out. The heritage that we bring from different lands is of extraordinary value, but our allegiance must be absolutely clear. This is the land and the people with whom we preserve its most cherished values. Any attempt to bypass that responsibility will bring destruction.

Does this mean that we will always see eye to eye? No. But is it not part of the greatness of this land that we have systems and structures in place to respect one another while providing civil ways of debate and change? Let us make no mistake about it. The murderers had only one passion. Hate. They had only one solution. Violence. The tragedy is that they have many in their footsteps. Civil people will have to come to grips with that reality. Our lifestyles will be changed because evil demands a response, and the response agonizes the tender conscience of good people. We have not seen the end of pain. It is part of the cost of caring and loving.

A second issue is religion and its political outworking. Freedom is a cherished ideal. Distributed liberty will always be vulnerable to the heinous acts of wicked men and women. That is the very reason the Christian and the Christian faith will always be vulnerable to abuse by those who seek to attack it. America, which could only have been framed from a Christian worldview, cannot make antiblasphemy laws, but Muslim nations and states can and do. There is a difference, and we had better be absolutely clear about it. The Christian cannot legitimately impose his faith across a land. But at the same time, we are given a unique privilege. In America no one need fear preaching the gospel and inviting men and women to trust in Jesus

Christ. The same cannot be said in many Islamic nations today. It is a fundamental difference in our commitment to freedom. The message of the gospel is not compulsion, but freedom.

In this lies a crossover between our politics and our faith. Just as the Christian is vulnerable to all kinds of mockery and abuse in the academy and the public square because there is no compulsion, so also the same possibilities exist for democracy to be abused in a religiously pluralistic society. Is it because democracy and Christianity are identical? No, it is because both share a fundamental tenet of self-determination. With that essential fact, we will always be open to plunder, disrespect, and attack by those who are determined to mock it. It is the price of freedom.

That being so, it is time for the moderate Muslims abroad to speak up. I hear a host of them denying any support of this dastardly act and trying to distance themselves from this criminal expression. We are deeply grateful to them for that. But in the same vein, they should openly condemn their Islamic nations that persecute, control, and kill Christians and those of other faiths. Numerous countries in the name of Islam have handcuffed Christians with severe limitations, even killing some for their faith. Why do these moderate Muslims not speak out? Where were they when Bishop Haik was tortured and murdered in Iran?

Where are they when ordinary Christians are terrorized by the application of the antiblasphemy law in Pakistan? I know of people today in prison who are brutalized in Islamic regimes. What may well be the underlying reality is not so much religion as it is power. If moderates are against such use of power, then let them publicly take a stand. In fact, their own peace-loving people are under the scourge of their demagogues. I have firsthand information that scores of people in Iran lit candles in their windows out of sympathy for those killed in this terrorist act, even though many were beaten and punished for this act. Why do not the Muslims overseas speak out against this evil? Until they do, their voices against terrorism will ring hollow, because the seeds of hate are sown long before they blossom to mass murder. Yes, there is a religious component, and it starts where the breeding ground exists.

The third is the spiritual reminder in this tragedy. The memorial service at the National Cathedral, which was planned by our president, will go down as one of the most moving moments in my life. I was alone in my room in Paris, engrossed in the proceedings. Hearing Billy Graham and our president drove me to my knees in gratitude that we have people of such sensitive hearts in places of leadership. Watching the closed eyes of members of Congress, Republican and Democrat alike, as they listened to the words of "The Lord's Prayer," reaffirmed in my heart what a great nation this is. And then to listen to the words of "A Mighty Fortress Is Our God" was a stirring reminder that devilish wills can never bring down His Word. Just as the cloud of hate unfurled by diabolical acts was dispelled by acts of mercy and love, so our pain and grief were brought to the Lord of all strength and healing.

One of the verses in that hymn says:

> *Did we in our own strength confide,*
> *Our striving would be losing;*
> *Were not the right man on our side,*
> *The man of God's own choosing:*
> *Dost ask who that may be?*
> *Christ Jesus it is He;*
> *Lord Sabbaoth His name,*
> *From age to age the same,*
> *And He must win the battle.*

This is a spiritual battle, and we must know both what we are up against and what our greatest strength must be. There is a pointed philosophical question that rises from the dust of thousands of graves. We must understand what we mean when we use morally condemning words to describe the slaughter. What do we mean by evil? Evil, simply and plainly, is the violation of purpose. Innocent people used as missiles. A passenger plane used as a weapon. Freedom used for its own destruction. Purpose was intrinsically violated, which means it is imperative to know what our purpose is as individuals and as a nation, else we will succumb to evil. We have before us as a nation the great and noble call to reconcile law with liberty. The ultimate moral law comes from God. The best expression of liberty is to reverence life. If we have no moral law and do not reverence life, then evil disappears in a cloud of self-serving acts. May we be clear in our souls that when we understand our purpose in keeping with our Creator, no diabolical intent will destroy that which God has said will truly set us free—knowing His Word and abiding in it.

The final component is the emotional strain on all of this. Seldom have I felt so alone. Sitting in a Thai hotel room, unable to call home, and watching the heinous act again and again brought me to tears. We have all needed an arm around us...yes, a human arm as well. We have needed the support and comfort of friends, and receiving it has been heartwarming. People all over the world have reached out to us. My Thai friends phoned me repeatedly in my room to express their sadness. The people of the United Kingdom have reached out with arms of love and comfort to every American. Tony Blair and his foreign secretary have minced no words. They will be there for us. Canada, France, Germany, Poland…the list is long. They share our values and shared in our grief. Their comfort will never be forgotten.

The psalmist wrote some despondent words three thousand years ago. They are found in Psalm 74. He describes his heart overwhelmed by grief when his enemies smashed everything that was sacred to him.

> *Your foes roared in the place*
> *where you met with us;*
> *they set up their standards as signs.*
>
> *They behaved like men wielding axes*
> *to cut through a thicket of trees.*
>
> *They smashed all the carved paneling*
> *with their axes and hatchets.*
>
> *They burned your sanctuary to the ground;*
> *they defiled the dwelling place of your Name.*
>
> *They said in their hearts*
> *"We will crush them completely!"*

In utter despair he mourned all that was lost and then said that there was no more voice in the land to help them know where the end of all of this was.

We can draw both a parallel and a contrast. Things we treasure have been plundered. But thank God we are not left without voices and without hope. On my way home, one flight attendant came and talked with me. When she found out what I did and my calling in life, she grabbed my hand and said, "Thanks for coming home." Another businessman, who stood in line next to me waiting to get a ticket, said halfway through our conversation, "I hope I get a seat next to you." Seldom have I seen such a desire to find spiritual hope in the midst of such grief. I happened to be in a famous cathedral in Paris the afternoon when Europe stood still for three minutes at midday to pray for America in her time of need. Even the famed Champs d'Elysees saw life come to a standstill during that time. Thousands were quiet or in prayer. In Psalm 73 we read the words: "When I tried to understand all this, it was too oppressive to me till I entered the sanctuary of God; then I understood their final destiny" (vv. 16–17). That sanctuary of the soul, no aircraft can destroy.

Those are sobering and comforting words. He who went to the cross gives us His own pillar of cloud and pillar of fire to protect and to lead us amidst the darkness with which doers of evil seek to blind us. May our churches bring hope and seriousness to what God wants of us as a people and as individuals. Only in Him can we find peace and confidence, knowing there is a destiny to which we all move.

How firm a foundation, ye saints of the Lord,
Is laid for your faith in His excellent Word!
What more can He say than to you He hath said,
To you who for refuge to Jesus have fled?

Fear not, I am with thee—O be not dismayed!
For I am thy God, and will still give thee aid;
I'll strengthen thee, help thee, and cause thee to stand,
Upheld by My righteous, omnipotent hand.

When through fiery trials thy pathway shall lie,
My grace, all-sufficient, shall be thy supply;
The flame shall not hurt thee—I only design
Thy dross to consume and thy gold to refine.

The soul that on Jesus hath leaned for repose,
I will not, I will not desert to his foes;
That soul, though all hell should endeavor to shake,
I'll never—no, never—no, never forsake![21]

Thank you for giving me a home here and for making me feel welcome.

Dear God, hear our prayer. Apart from You we have no hope.

Notes

1. Kai Neilsen, "Why Should I Be Moral?" *American Philosophical Quarterly* 21 (1984): 90.

2. Richard Dawkins, *Out of Eden* (New York: Basic Books, 1992), 133.

3. Arthur Jeffrey, *Islam: Muhammad and His Religion* (New York: The Library of Liberal Arts, 1982), 66.

4. See Surah 2.106.

5. John Gilchrist, *Muhammad and the Religion of Islam* (Geoffrey St., Roodepoort, Republic of South Africa: Mission Press, 1986), 44.

6. R. Bosworth-Smith, *Mohammed and Mohammedanism* (London, U.K.: Smith, Elder & Co., 1876) 138.

7. John Gilchrist, *Muhammad and the Religion of Islam,* 65.

8. I recommend the article "What Is the Koran?" in the January 1999 *Atlantic Monthly.* That article is an eye-opener and underscores the war behind the battles.

9. Their works are still available and provide an open window to what is at stake here. Abu Zaid's *The Concept of the Text* and Ali Dashti's *Twenty-Three Years: A Study of the Prophetic Career of Mohammed* are profound books, definitely worth reading.

10. Hasan al-Banna,"Five Tracts of Hasan al-Banna," trans. Charles Wendell (Berkley, Calif.: University of California Press, 1978) 80, 82.

11. "A Moment of Crisis," *20/20,* October 1982.

12. Muqtedar Khan "A Memo to American Muslims," *Ijtihad*, http://www.ijtihad.org/memo.htm.

13. Elias Chacour has written a moving account of this aspect of the conflict. The book is called *Blood Brothers*, for that is what they are.

14. Thomas V. Morris, *Making Sense of It All* (Grand Rapids, Mich.: Eerdmans Publishing Company, 1992) 93.

15. Henri Nouwen, *The Only Necessary Thing* (New York: Crossroads Publishing Co., 1999) 30.

16. Ibid., n.p.

17. Andrew Sullivan, "This Is a Religious War," *The New York Times Magazine*, 7 October 2001, n.p.

18. I have written about the philosophical bankruptcy of secularism elsewhere, so I will not discuss it here. For further reading see *Can Man Live without God* (Dallas, Tex.: Word Publishing, 1994); *Deliver Us from Evil* (Dallas, Tex.: Word Publishing, 1996).

19. Jim McLean, "The Massacre of Glencoe." Words and music by Jim McLean. Published by Duart Music, 1963. Used by permission.

20. Henri Nouwen, *The Only Necessary Thing*, 14.

21. John Rippon , comp., *A Selection of Hymns from the Best Authors* (London: 1787). From "How Firm a Foundation.

The publisher and author would love
to hear your comments about this book.

PLEASE CONTACT US AT:
www.multnomah.net/jihad

STEP INTO A "LONG-TAIL" BOAT ON THE RIVER OF KINGS

...and become immersed in an imaginary conversation between Jesus Christ and Gautama Buddha.

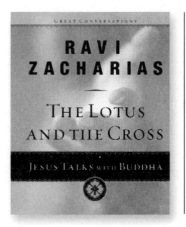

"This captivating dialogue not only clears up confusion about the claims of Christ and Buddha, it provides us with a highly entertaining read."

—CHUCK COLSON

"...this unique drama will educate, enthrall, and enlighten you—and everyone you share it with for years to come."

—BRUCE WILKINSON, author of the *NY Times* #1 bestseller *The Prayer of Jabez*

- Both talked about the "self," but one denied it even existed.
- Both felt the pain of human suffering, but each had radically different responses to it.
- Both addressed our deepest hungers, but one saw them as an impediment, the other as a clue.
- Both have earned a worldwide following—but their answers are worlds apart.

Jesus and Buddha agreed that Truth could withstand scrutiny. Listen in as the Soul of Truth speaks with the Heart of Compassion. It could change your life.

ISBN 1-57673-854-X